Group's® Best JR. HIGH MEETINGS

VOLUME TWO

Edited by
Michael D. Warden

Group® Books

Loveland, Colorado

Group's Best Jr. High Meetings, Volume 2

Credits
Edited by Michael D. Warden
Book and Cover Design by Judy Atwood Bienick

Scripture quotations are from the Holy Bible, New International Version. Copyright © 1973, 1978, 1984 International Bible Society. Used by permission of Zondervan Bible Publishers.

Library of Congress Cataloging-in-Publication Data
Group's best jr. high meetings.
 Selections from Group's jr. high ministry magazine.
 ISBN 0-931529-58-1 (pbk. Vol. 1)
 Vol. 2- : edited by Michael D. Warden.
 Warden, Michael D.
 1. Church work with teenagers. I. Parolini, Cindy, 1960- . II. Group's jr. high ministry.
III. Group's best jr. high meetings.
BV4447.G695 1987   268'.433   87-8591

15 14 13 12 11 10 9 8   04 03 02 01 00 99 98 97

ISBN 1-55945-009-6   **Group's Best Jr. High Meetings, Volume 2**
Printed in the United States of America.

Contents

How to Use This Book 5

SECTION ONE: *SELF-IMAGE*

1. Becoming the Me I Want to Be 9
Polish the traits that will help you be a better person

2. Discovering How God Sees Me 17
See yourself in a new way

3. Me? A Gift? 23
Discover how you are a gift from God to others

4. Temples Under Construction 28
Put feelings about your body into perspective

SECTION TWO: *FRIENDSHIP*

5. Friends: Help or Hindrance? 37
Evaluate your friendships

6. Please Like Me 45
Find positive ways to seek others' acceptance

Special Series: Coping With Peer Pressure

7. The Truth About Peer Pressure 52
Discover how peer pressure happens

8. From Bad News to Good News 59
Deal positively with negative peer pressure

9. You Can Do It! 65
Learn to stand alone when you have to

SECTION THREE: *FAMILY*

10. Growing Up 74
Learn the relationship between freedom and responsibility

11. Family Feelings 81
See how other families work

12. A Family-Ties Surprise 88
See things from your parents' perspective

13. Why Do My Parents Embarrass Me? 96
Learn how to deal with embarrassing situations

SECTION FOUR: *FAITH*

14. Does God Really Love Me? 103
Understand God's unconditional love

15. Getting to Know God 109
Grow more intimate with God

16. Hunting for God's Will 116
Apply God's will to your everyday life

17. **Jesus Power** **122**
Rest in God's care and protection

18. **Ups and Downs of Faith** **129**
Find help through the changes in your faith

19. **What to Do When God Says No** **135**
Discover the real purpose of prayer

SECTION FIVE: *ISSUES*

20. **Facing Death** **142**
See death from God's perspective

21. **Jesus vs. Rambo** **148**
Discover the effects of violence on your attitude

22. **Managing Your Moods** **154**
Control how you react to your feelings

23. **Understanding AIDS** **161**
Share feelings about AIDS

24. **What's So Important About Grades?** **169**
Put grades in perspective

25. **When Stress Weighs You Down** **176**
Grow from stress

SECTION SIX: *VALUES AND DECISIONS*

26. **Cheating** **182**
Understand the negative effects of cheating

Special Series: Drugs, Alcohol and Junior Highers

27. **Exploring the Facts** **189**
Discuss concerns about drugs and alcohol

28. **Clarifying Values** **196**
See how drugs and alcohol affect your life

29. **Facing Peer Pressure** **202**
Say no to drugs and alcohol

---

30. **Lying** **209**
Tell the truth no matter what

31. **Risky Business** **215**
Take a hard look at risky behavior

32. **TV and Me** **221**
See how television shapes your perspective

Special Series: Sex Is for Marriage

33. **Instructions Included** **229**
Discover God's view of sex

34. **Warning! Contents Could Explode** **236**
Make wise decisions about sexual behavior

35. **Fragile: Handle With Care** **242**
Say no to premarital sex

How to Use This Book

Welcome to the second collection of the best meetings from Group's JR. HIGH MINISTRY Magazine!

Welcome to the adventure of sharing meaningful growth experiences with junior highers!

We all know that leading young teenagers to Christian maturity is a challenging task. Junior high kids are just beginning to move from concrete to abstract thinking. And generally speaking, faith speaks an abstract language.

Here's help. These faith-stretching meetings start where junior highers are. They tie Christian principles to everyday, concrete moorings. These meetings effectively:

● challenge young people to live their Christian faith—and show them how;

● channel junior highers' energy into creative and involving activities; and

● give you step-by-step guidelines for successful learning experiences with junior highers.

Each meeting spells out its objectives, and lists everything you need to prepare. Each session also provides easy-to-use handouts (which you have permission to copy).

Junior high leaders across the country contributed these meetings. And thousands have used them with junior highers. They find that the programs work well for Sunday school or fellowship meetings. Some even adapt the meetings to retreat schedules.

So join the crowd. Let *your* junior highers enjoy the world of relational, experiential learning about their faith.

Choosing Which Meetings to Use

Where to start? Begin by asking kids what their needs are; do an informal phone survey or a full-blown written survey. Where do your junior highers want help? In areas of self-image? Getting along with family? Keeping friends? Standing up to peer pressure? Let them tell you.

One excellent resource for determining your kids' needs is *Determining Needs in Your Youth Ministry* by Peter L. Benson and Dorothy L. Williams (Group Books). This book provides all you need to do a detailed survey of your young people's needs.

Map out your plan for meetings two or more months in advance. Include meetings on the topics your junior highers name. (If they name a topic

6 you don't find in this volume, send us a note so we can cover it in Group's JR. HIGH MINISTRY Magazine.) Also include in your plans the three special series in this book:

● Coping With Peer Pressure;

● Drugs, Alcohol and Junior Highers; and

● Sex Is for Marriage.

Aim for balance. Don't do all three of the series consecutively. Spatter them between meetings on self-image or family relationships. And realize that while the meetings in the "Faith" section have faith issues as their starting points, *all* the meetings apply faith to life.

Once you've mapped your plan, be flexible. You may carefully prepare for the "Family Feelings" meeting and then discover that your junior highers are quietly panicking about tests they're facing at school. Switch gears. Do the "What's So Important About Grades?" meeting. You'll give kids a stronger message of love by caring enough to meet their needs—even when it's inconvenient—than by following through on your original plan.

Adapting the Meetings for Your Group

Make these meetings your own. Adapt them to fit your group and your style. For example:

● If you always begin your junior high meetings with a game of volleyball, by all means begin these meetings with volleyball. Or singing. Or announcements. Or (yes, even) refreshments. Ritual is important.

● The meetings use both large and small groups. If your group is large, divide into small groups for discussions and projects. But if your group's small,

you're all set—just ignore the notes to create small groups.

● Adapt the supplies as necessary. For example, the meetings often list newsprint and markers. Save money by using a chalkboard.

Planning for the Meetings

Some nuts-and-bolts tips to help you plan smooth-running meetings:

● Familiarize yourself with the scripture passages used in the meetings.

● Imagine the impact a particular meeting can have in specific junior highers' lives. Pray for a meaningful, growth-filled time together.

● For excitement, choose a variety of meeting places. Do the "Facing Death" meeting in a cemetery. Do the "Understanding AIDS" meeting at a hospital. Do "Family Feelings" in a junior higher's family room at home.

● Get adult sponsors and leader-type kids involved in preparing and leading meetings. Meet together to divide responsibilities such as collecting supplies, doing "Before the Meeting" tasks, setting up the meeting area or distributing items during the meetings. Some junior highers may even be able to lead parts of your meetings.

● Plan specific time slots for the activities. Jot the times on a 3×5 card or right in this book to help keep you on track. The meetings generally fit nicely into either a 60-minute or 90-minute time slot, depending on how much time you spend on the games and crowdbreakers. Or how large your group is.

● Don't underestimate prizes. It's amazing how hard junior highers will work for even a small reward.

● Remember refreshments. Again, meetings generally don't include snack ideas unless they relate to the theme or incorporate a needed break. But you know junior highers!

Running the Meetings

Meeting time. The supplies are in order, the kids and adult sponsors are arriving. Go for it—keeping these things in mind:

● Greet everyone with a positive attitude and an upbeat setting. Some meetings say to have contemporary Christian music playing (especially when it relates to the theme). Why not play Christian music at the beginning of all get-togethers?

● When dividing the group for small group discussions, include an adult sponsor in each group. Meetings on difficult topics such as sexuality or drug use require an adult in each group.

● Use adult sponsors to fill in as necessary when you divide the group into pairs.

● In all discussions, remain open and honest with junior highers. You can only expect your kids to be honest and vulnerable if you and other adults show the way. On the other hand, don't force sharing or get too intense too fast.

● Be on the lookout for any kids who don't receive their share of affirmation notes (or whatever) in an activity. Have a couple of adult sponsors or leader-type kids watching too; they can take action themselves as well as encourage others to fill in the gaps.

● Rearrange your time schedule if necessary. You may find kids seriously dealing with an activity you had expected to be a simple, quick crowdbreaker. Rather than stop the learning, change your time slot from five minutes to 15.

● And, yes, when the worst happens and an activity flops, don't fret. In the first place, you may never really know what the kids got out of it. And in the second place, every "failure" has learnings in it. Seek them out with your group members. Analyze why something didn't work like you had in mind. Change it a bit and try again. Turn a disappointment into an adventure.

Following Through

One benefit of meetings that use concrete objects to carry the messages is that learning continues long after the lessons end. Every time your junior highers see a gift-wrapped package after experiencing the "Me? A Gift?" meeting, they'll remember to be thankful for God's love; or every time they see a feather floating through the air, they'll reflect on how even "white" lies can go too far to ever be taken back.

Here are some deliberate things you can do to help the meetings' impact remain in your kids' lives:

● Encourage junior highers to take the meetings beyond the (church) walls by taking home handouts or creations.

● At times you may want to keep for yourself completed worksheets that you feel give valuable insight about particular kids.

● Set times to meet with kids who express special needs or concerns during the meetings. Get together for soft drinks after school and talk.

● Meet with adult sponsors after meetings to swap insights about kids.

● Refer to previous meetings to reinforce the learning and keep the meeting lessons alive.

Section One:

SELF-IMAGE

1 Becoming the Me I Want to Be

By Katie Abercrombie

They're changing fast, these junior highers. Just about the time they're waving goodbye to elementary school, they begin to think about who they are and how other people see them. So they try on different roles and personalities to see which fit them best.

This process can be confusing to adults who work with junior highers. Even the kids are confused about it. They see themselves, and their friends, changing so fast that insecurity becomes a normal state.

Use this meeting to help junior highers think about who they are and who they want to be.

OBJECTIVES

Participants will:
- begin to think about the personality characteristics that make up who they are;
- imagine themselves as "diamonds in the rough" being polished into brilliance by expectations of self, friends, parents and God;
- evaluate which personality traits they want to polish away and which they want to shine more brightly; and
- think about how they want to shine in the future.

10 BEFORE THE MEETING

Read the meeting, collect supplies and photocopy handouts. Ask several kids to prepare and bring refreshments for the meeting. Using posterboard or heavy construction paper, cut out a sample diamond similar to the drawing below. Make it about the size of a Frisbee. Draw the lines as illustrated. Write your name in the top center section and in each of the remaining sections write one of your personal characteristics.

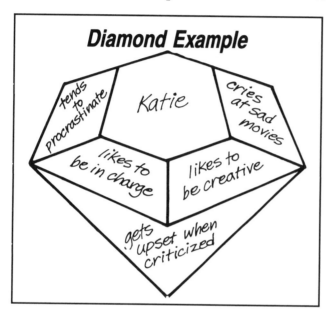

Diamond Example

Make four diamond-shape signs out of posterboard. Write one of the following on each: Self, Friends, Parents, God. Tape one sign in the middle of each of the four walls in the meeting room. Put a table for supplies near each sign. The signs mark the locations for the stations in the Who polishes me? activity.

Recruit four volunteers to guide kids at each of the Who polishes me? stations.

Buy enough plastic diamonds from a craft store for each group member to have one, or have kids help you make diamonds from foil or construction paper.

THE MEETING

1. Diamond name tags—(You'll need four or five different colors of posterboard or heavy construction paper, scissors, markers, yarn, pencils, hole punchers and your sample diamond.) As kids arrive, show them your sample diamond and have each person make a similar diamond.

Say: **Write your name in the top center section of your diamond and write characteristics that describe your personality in each of the other sections. For example, if you always get worried before tests, write that. Or if you like being with lots of people, write that. Don't write things like "Green is my favorite color" or "I hate spinach." If you have trouble thinking of things to write, think about how your friends, parents or teachers describe you. After you're done writing, punch two holes in the top of your** diamond, attach a piece of yarn and wear it around your neck.

2. *Diamond tag*—Form pairs by asking kids each to link elbows with one person who's wearing the same-color diamond as they are.

Say: **Form a circle of pairs leaving one pair outside the circle. Pairs in the circle should keep arms linked with their partners, but not with other pairs in the circle. The "left out" pair should unlink arms and decide who will be the "Chaser" and who will be the "Chased." Chaser chases Chased around the circle of pairs. Chased may run around and through the circle, but not out of the immediate area of the group. If Chaser tags Chased, they change roles. Chased can avoid being tagged by linking elbows with the free arm of one member of one of the pairs. The other member of that pair then becomes Chased and must run and/or link arms with someone else.**

Play Diamond Tag for at least five minutes, then stop the game and ask pairs with linked arms to sit down facing their partners. Chased and Chaser should also pair up. Ask partners to explain the things written on their diamonds. Have them each tell why a certain characteristic—like "Laughs at silly cartoons"— is important to their personality.

3. *People diamonds*—(You'll need the "People Diamonds" statements on page 12 to read aloud.) Gather the group together. Say: **Most people wonder at times if they're the person they want to be. But junior highers probably wonder about that more than anyone. You may have just started to ask yourself who you really want to be. Personality characteristics help us define who that "me" really is. So we're going to do something that will help each of us find who the "me" inside is, and see how others see themselves.**

I'll read some statements that have two possible endings. Listen to the statements and choose the one ending that best describes you. If you choose the first ending, move to the right side of the room. If you choose the second ending, move to the left side of the room.

Form discussion groups on both sides of the room after you read each statement. Call out a number once kids have made their choice, and have them form a "people diamond" of that

12

People Diamonds

1. I'm always . . .
   - on time.
   - running late.

2. I prefer snacks that are . . .
   - sweet.
   - salty.

3. I enjoy friendships that are . . .
   - few and long-lasting.
   - numerous and changing.

4. I like being with people who are . . .
   - talkative.
   - more interested in listening to me.

5. At a party or group event, I like to . . .
   - meet and talk to lots of people.
   - hang around with people I know well.

6. I believe in . . .
   - punishing people who break the law.
   - giving lawbreakers another chance.

7. I like to . . .
   - dream big dreams.
   - focus on what is real.

8. I usually . . .
   - do things the same way as everyone else.
   - do things my own way.

9. I study better . . .
   - alone.
   - with friends.

10. At a sad movie, I'm more likely to . . .
    - cry.
    - laugh.

11. I like things to happen . . .
    - by chance.
    - as planned.

12. I think of myself as . . .
    - tenderhearted.
    - levelheaded.

13. I usually . . .
    - see the best in a situation.
    - see the worst in a situation.

number with other kids who've made the same choice. For example, if you call out "two," kids should form pairs. If time is short, only call out a number every third or fourth question. Once kids form their people diamonds, ask them to tell each other why they chose that particular ending to the statement.

Read the statements and allow time for discussion.

Ask kids what they learned about themselves through this activity.

4. Who polishes me?—(You'll need to set up the four Who polishes me? stations according to the station instructions on page 15. You'll also need tape or yarn, and a copy of the station instructions for each volunteer. Gather the group together. Say: **Our personalities are shaped by what we expect of ourselves as well as what others expect of us. Often these expectations conflict. But as we grow, we learn to respond to expectations we think are worthwhile. We work to fulfill them.**

The four diamonds you see on the walls are the sources of most expectations. Under each diamond sign is a station where you'll work on a project that's related to the expectations others have of you. A volunteer at each station will explain how to complete the activity.

Form four groups and assign each group to one of the stations. Allow 10 minutes for each group to complete its project. Then have kids form pairs to talk about their finished projects. After a minute or two, move each group on to the next station. When everyone has been to each station, ask kids each to attach all four of their projects in a chain using tape or yarn. Display their projects on a table or wall.

Gather the group together and ask:

● **What expectations are you looking forward to fulfilling? Why?**

● **What expectations make you scared or angry? Why?**

● **How are your expectations of yourself similar to others' expectations of you? different from others' expectations? Explain.**

Read aloud Matthew 6:25-34. Say: **Jesus understands how you feel about all these expectations, and he's promised to help. He'll give you peace if you seek him first.**

5. *Mining for diamonds*—(For every two kids you'll need a posterboard "Bible Diamond" with one of the following Bible verses on each one: Galatians 5:16-26; Ephesians 4:17-32; Philippians 2:1-18; Colossians 3:12-17; 1 Thessalonians 5:12-24. For every two kids you'll also need a Bible, a marker, five to 10 white construction paper diamonds, five to 10 gray construction paper coal pieces and tape.) Gather the group together. Say: **When people mine for diamonds, they keep the uncut stones and throw away less valuable stuff such as coal. God shows us through the Bible which characteristics are like diamonds—ones we should keep and value—and which characteristics are like coal—ones we should throw away.**

14

Ask kids to get together with their original partners from the Diamond Tag game. Give each pair a Bible, a Bible Diamond, a set of blank white diamonds, a set of blank gray coal pieces and a marker.

Say: **Find the verse listed on your Bible Diamond and read it with your partner. On each blank diamond, write one characteristic God wants us to have or keep. On each piece of coal, write one characteristic God wants us to throw away. When you're finished, tape your diamonds and coal on the wall and look at what others have taped up.**

Gather the group back together and ask:
● **How do you acquire diamond characteristics?**
● **How do you get rid of coal characteristics?**

6. *Shining and polishing*—(You'll need a marker for each person.) Have kids get back together with their partners from the Mining for Diamonds Bible study.

Say: **Think of yourself as a diamond. Which characteristics would you like to polish away, and which ones would you like to shine brighter? When you decide, turn your name tag over and write one thing about yourself you'd like to polish away and one thing you'd like to shine brighter. Then with your partner talk about what you wrote.**

7. *Closing*—(You'll need plastic, foil or construction paper diamonds.) Gather everyone into a circle with partners standing next to each other. Pass out one "diamond" to each person. Ask kids each to think of at least one "facet" of their partner's personality they appreciate. Then have kids, one at a time, each give their partner a diamond and tell him or her what facet(s) they appreciate. Then close with a prayer thanking God for making everyone shine more brightly.

8. *Refreshments*—(You'll need the snacks kids have prepared.) Celebrate with multifaceted refreshments.

Who Polishes Me?
Station Instructions

Instructions: Go over these instructions with your station volunteers, and ask them to explain each project carefully to kids.

Self—(You'll need magazines, scissors, tape or glue and large diamond-shape pieces of posterboard or heavy construction paper.) Have kids think about the expectations they have of themselves. Ask:
- **What do you want to be like?**
- **How would you like other people to describe you?**
- **Are you a caring person?**
- **Can your friends count on you in a crisis?**
- **Are you someone people can trust?**

Say: **Don't think so much of external achievements such as good grades or top athlete. Using the magazines, cut out words and pictures that describe who you'd like to be. Then glue or tape them to your posterboard diamond.**

Friends—(You'll need pipe cleaners, construction paper, tape or glue and large diamond-shape pieces of posterboard or heavy construction paper.) Have kids think of the expectations their friends have of them. Ask:
- **Are you a good listener?**
- **Do you tell funny jokes?**
- **Are you up on the latest fashions?**
- **Are you loyal or are you a fair-weather friend?**

Say: **Once you've thought of some things your friends expect of you, use pipe cleaners and construction paper to build a model of the person your friends expect you to be. For example, if your friends always expect you to be witty and funny, make your pipe-cleaner model doubled over in laughter.
When you're finished, attach your model to your posterboard diamond.**

Parents—(You'll need markers and large diamond-shape pieces of posterboard or heavy construction paper.) Have kids think about expectations their parents have of them. Ask:
- **What personality characteristics do your parents hope you'll develop— responsibility, helpfulness, resourcefulness, kindness, perseverance?**

continued

16

Say: **Write your first name across the middle of your posterboard diamond. Then write some of your parents' expectations of you vertically, so they intersect your name at a common letter. Write one characteristic for each letter in your name. For example:**

```
                h
                o
                n            k
                e     f      i
        S   u   s  a  n
                i     n      t
                t     d      i  d
                n     t
                c     e      h
                e     r      f
                r     s      u
                e     t      l
                      a
                      n
                      d
                      i
                      n
                      g
```

God—(You'll need clay, paper clips and large diamond-shape pieces of posterboard or heavy construction paper.) Have kids think about the expectations God has of them. Ask:
● **What characteristics does God want you to develop?**
● **What kind of person pleases him most?**
● **Are you learning to love others the way God loves you?**
● **Are you trying to follow Jesus' steps or someone else's?**
Say: **Now take some clay and make a model of a characteristic that God would like you to have. For example, if God wants you to be more loving, make a clay heart. Or if he wants you to be more rooted in the Bible, make a tree. When you're finished, attach your model to your posterboard diamond using paper clips.**

2 Discovering How God Sees Me

By Dr. Larry Keefauver

According to Search Institute's study of early adolescents, 82 percent of ninth-grade girls say it's very important "to feel good about myself." Another 33 percent say they spend a lot of time thinking about their identity. Two out of five say they have negative feelings about how their bodies look to others.

Use this meeting to help kids discover and appreciate each other's uniqueness. Help them learn to build new and honest relationships with one another by looking at themselves through God's eyes.

OBJECTIVES

Participants will:

● get to know one another by understanding how they see themselves and one another;

● compare their self-image with how others view them;

● understand more fully God's image of them; and

● give and receive positive feedback about each other's unique personality traits.

BEFORE THE MEETING

Read the meeting, collect supplies and photocopy handouts. For each person, cut out of over-size construction paper an

18

equilateral triangle with 12-inch sides.

Print each of the Bible passages and statements from the "God's-Eye View" box on a separate sheet of newsprint and tape them on walls around the meeting room.

Find an instant-print camera and get enough film to take a picture of each person.

THE MEETING

1. *God's good creation*—(For every two people you'll need newsprint and two markers.) As kids arrive, form pairs and give each pair a sheet of newsprint and two markers. Say: **God's creation reflects his character. Just as you can be identified by your fingerprints, God has left his "fingerprints" in the world he created. If you look closely enough, you can see God in the world around you.**

Partners, spread your newsprint horizontally and write your names at the top. Underneath your names, print the following five words, leaving space between each word: Seeing, Hearing, Touching, Smelling and Tasting. Then under each word, list things you enjoy about God's creation that relate to that sense. For example, I love the smell of rain, so I would write "Rain" under Smelling.

When pairs finish, have them each write at the bottom of their newsprint: "God saw all that he had made, including (their names), and it was very good!" Gather together and ask pairs to explain their responses.

2. *Mystery identities*—(For each person you'll need two pieces of paper and a pencil.) Form a circle, hand out paper and pencils, and ask kids each to write a description of themselves without describing how they look. Ask them to write about their personality qualities, how they treat others, what they like and dislike, their future goals and their relationship with God. Caution them not to use their names or provide details about their families or where they live. Have kids each fold their description and pass it to you.

Write a number at the top of each description. Have kids each number a piece of paper starting with "1" and ending with the number of kids present. Read aloud each numbered description; then ask kids to write who they think the description fits.

Ask kids each to say which description (by number) is theirs.

Have kids check their answers. Ask:
  ● **How do others see you differently from the way you see yourself?**
  ● **How willing are you to let others see you as you really are?**
  ● **If people expect you to be a certain way, do you try to meet their expectations? Why or why not?**
  ● **What do you risk when you allow someone to see your true self?**

3. *A God's-eye view of me*—(You'll need a copy of the "God's-Eye View" sheet with scriptures and corresponding statements cut apart and taped separately on your meeting room walls. For every two people you'll need a construction paper triangle and a Bible. For every person you'll need a 3×5 card and a pencil.) Have kids each find the same partner they had in activity #1. Give each pair a construction paper triangle and a Bible.

Say: **With your partner, go around the room and look up the scripture passage that's on each piece of paper on the wall. After you read the scripture, discuss with your partner what qualities God has given us that are like him. Then decide which of the statements are true and which are false. Write the true statements on your triangle. When you've finished every God's-Eye View passage, tape your triangle on the wall.**

Give everyone a 3×5 card. Ask kids each to answer on their 3×5 card the following questions. Ask:
  ● **What's one thing, positive or negative, that God sees in me that I've failed to see in myself?**
  ● **What's one way others see me that's similar to the way God sees me?**
  ● **What's one way others see me that's different from the way God sees me?**
  ● **What's one negative idea about God I'm ready to give up?**
  ● **What's one negative belief about myself I'm ready to give up?**
When kids finish answering the questions, give them a moment to think about their answers, and then ask them to keep their 3×5 cards as reminders.

4. *Here's to you!*—(You'll need an instant-print camera with enough film to take one picture of each person. For each person

20

God's-Eye View

Instructions: Cut apart each section and tape on your meeting room walls.

Genesis 1:27-31

- God created me good.
- God created me and then broke the mold.
- God created me to sin and fail.
- God created me to help take care of the Earth.
- God created me to use the Earth the way I want to.

Psalm 8:4-8

- God created me and then forgot me.
- God cares for the Earth more than he cares for me.
- God created me special.
- God created me to be clothed with glory and honor.

continued

Psalm 139:13-16

- God created me but made some mistakes in the process.
- God created me wonderful, inside and out.
- God knew me from the moment I was conceived.
- God knows my every thought and feeling.
- God has a wonderful plan for my life.
- God doesn't know or care about my future.

2 Corinthians 5:17

- God is doing something new in my life.
- God can change me now and can continue to change me the rest of my life.
- God makes me a new person so I can forget and forgive things I've done in the past.
- God will punish me for my past for the rest of my life.

22

you'll need a piece of paper and scissors.) Have kids form a circle. Ask kids each to trace their hand on paper. Then have them each cut out their sketch, write their name across the bottom and "One thing God and I appreciate about you is . . ." across the top. Say: **As we pass the hand prints around, write one thing you appreciate about each person.**

After the hand prints have all been passed around, give kids a few moments to read what others have written. Then take an instant-print picture of each person and ask kids to each write on the bottom of their picture the following: "My prayer request is that God would help me improve my self-image by . . ."

Have kids find their partners again and exchange pictures. Have partners each pray silently for the other's prayer request and keep the picture for a daily prayer reminder. Form a circle and close by singing a favorite song.

3 Me? A Gift?

By Joani Schultz

A *poor self-image probably plagues a junior higher more than anything else: "I can't do anything right." "I don't matter to anybody." "I hate myself." "I wish I were somebody else."*

Thoughts like these affect how kids act. And what they believe about God and themselves.

Use this meeting to help junior highers know they're unique, valuable gifts from God.

OBJECTIVES

Participants will:

● experience "gift" games to build excitement toward the theme;

● tell their view of themselves as gifts;

● read, draw and discuss scripture that expresses their self-worth; and

● each set one goal for "giving themselves away" as gifts.

BEFORE THE MEETING

Read the meeting and collect supplies.

Recall times you felt worthless and times you felt like a gift. Be willing to tell others about those times. Pray that your junior highers each will understand their unique value and grow in appreciation of God's love.

For activity #1, gather three gift-wrapped prizes labeled one through three that can be shared; for example, candy, fruit and gum. Also gather cassette tapes or records of Christmas music and a cassette or record player.

24

For activity #3, gather one large box for every four people—large enough for a person to stand inside. Cover each box with newsprint or plain paper.

For activities #7 and #8, photocopy and cut apart the "Gift Tag" page so that each person has a gift tag. Provide 2-foot pieces of yarn so kids each can hang their tag around their neck.

THE MEETING

1. *Guess the gifts*—(You'll need a recording of Christmas music and equipment to play it on. You'll also need three gift-wrapped prizes labeled one through three. For each person you'll need a slip of paper and a pencil.) Play Christmas music as kids arrive. Display three wrapped gifts numbered from one to three. Give kids each a slip of paper and a pencil. Encourage them to guess what's in each package by writing their guesses, numbered one through three. Announce the winners at the end of the meeting and award the gifts to whoever guessed correctly on the most gifts.

2. *Human gift wrap*—(For each team, you'll need newspapers, masking tape and ribbon.) Form teams of four. Have teams each choose one person who'll be their gift. On "go," teams must wrap the gift person in newspapers using masking tape and ribbon. After five minutes (or when teams are finished) have all the wrapped gifts stand together while everyone applauds and cheers.

3. *Gift rap*—(For each team you'll need a large box and assorted markers.) After the "gifts" get unwrapped, gather the group in a circle. Say: **We've played some games that point to our meeting's theme: You are a gift. Most of the time we might not feel like a gift. We might even feel worthless, stupid, untalented; some of us might think we don't have a reason to live. But we do. During our time together we're going to explore our feelings about ourselves and then see what God thinks of us.**

To do that, each team will receive a giant gift box and markers. I'll tell you what to do as we go along.

Instruct each team to sit around its box so each person faces one side of the box. First explain they'll each be designing award-winning gift wrap by decorating their side of the box with symbols you'll explain to them. Have kids each write their name in the center of their box side. Have them surround their name with words that describe them that start with the same letters in their name.

Say: **In the upper left-hand corner, draw a picture that illustrates this sentence completion: "I feel worthless when . . ."** (Allow a few minutes, then continue.) **In the upper right-hand corner, draw a picture that illustrates this sentence completion: "I feel like a gift to the world when . . ."**

Beginning with the person on each team who was gift-wrapped, have team members each explain to their teammates reasons for what they've drawn. Tell teams to gather around the person who's explaining so they can all see what was drawn.

Giant Gift Example

4. *Gift words*—(You'll need a sheet of newsprint with these references on it taped on the wall: Genesis 1:27-31; Psalm 139:1-14; Matthew 5:14-16; 6:25-34; John 3:16; 15:12-16; Romans 8:38-39; 1 Corinthians 12:27; Ephesians 2:4-10; 1 Peter 2:9. For each person you'll need a Bible and a marker.)

Say: **From these verses, choose seven key words or phrases that tell you you're a gift. On your side of the box, illustrate or decorate each word or phrase to complete your award-winning gift wrap.**

When everyone's finished, have kids explain their box-side masterpieces to their teammates. Encourage some to tell the whole group about their gift words.

5. *You're a gift*—Have teams each select the person on their team whose clothes most resemble gift wrap. Have that person stand in the box while teammates tell him or her "You're a gift to me and others because . . ." Then have team members take turns getting into the box and receiving affirmation until everyone has.

6. *Gift stack*—When teams finish, have them show off their gift boxes. Bring all the boxes together to create a gift sculpture such as a pyramid or tower.

26

7. *Gift goals*—(For each person, you'll need a gift tag and a pencil.) Gather the group in a circle and give each person a gift tag and a pencil.

Gift Tag Example

TO:
FROM:
MY GIFT:

Tell junior highers to fill out their gift tags. Explain that "To" means a specific person they plan to reach out to. "From" means they each need to write their own name. And "My Gift" is what kids each specifically plan to do to be a gift. For example, "To Mom, From Penny, My Gift is to hug you when I get home, and clean my room on Saturday." Have kids tell one other person their goal.

8. *Gift send-off*—(You'll need the gift-wrapped prizes used in activity #1.) Have kids place their gift tags around their necks, stand in a circle and join hands. Explain that this prayer will be one of thankfulness and encouragement for the people in the group.

Say: **For the gift of (name) . . .**

Then have the group respond: "We give God thanks!" Have whoever is mentioned place one hand palm-down in the center of their circle. As others are mentioned, have them each pile their hand on top. Randomly say kids' names until everyone's included. When all group members have their hands in the center, they'll resemble a team huddle. So conclude the prayer with "Go, gifts, go!"

Don't forget to award the prizes for the guesses. Make sure the prizes are shared as a closing snack.

Gift Tag

Instructions: Photocopy these tags, cut them apart and give one to each volunteer.

TO:
FROM:
MY GIFT:

TO:
FROM:
MY GIFT:

TO:
FROM:
MY GIFT:

TO:
FROM:
MY GIFT:

TO:
FROM:
MY GIFT:

TO:
FROM:
MY GIFT:

4 Temples Under Construction

By Katie Abercrombie

Kids' self-esteem often plunges when they enter adolescence. Much of the drop is due to two things: rapid bodily changes and obsessive comparison of themselves with others. They become overly critical of the way they look. And many feel they simply can't measure up to the physical standards they've set for themselves.

God's view of kids and their changing, sometimes awkward-looking bodies runs counter to society's standards. King David knew the truth when he wrote: "I praise you because I am fearfully and wonderfully made; your works are wonderful, I know that full well" (Psalm 139:14).

Use this meeting to help your junior highers see themselves as "God's temples" under construction.

OBJECTIVES

Participants will:

● discuss the changes they experience as they move through adolescence;

● discover that everyone goes through similar changes at their age;

● learn ways they can be more responsible for their own well-being;

● see how society influences their physical expectations; and

● understand God's perspective of their bodies.

BEFORE THE MEETING

Read the meeting, collect supplies and photocopy handouts.

If you decide to use a weight chart for activity #5, ask your doctor for one.

Ask parents to provide healthy "temple-building" snacks for your post-meeting celebration.

THE MEETING

1. *Balloon people*—(For each person you'll need at least two long, skinny balloons of the same color, string, scissors, construction paper, markers and tape.) As kids arrive give them each at least two balloons, string and scissors. Say: **Blow up your balloons and twist them into the shape of a person. Then cut a piece of string, tie both ends to your balloon person, and hang it around your neck.** (See the "Balloon Person Example.")

Have kids each pick a piece of construction paper. Tell them each to cut out a shape that best describes how they feel about themselves. For example, kids could use a question mark because they're unsure of themselves, or a duck because they sometimes feel awkward.

Ask kids each to write their name on their shape and tape it on their balloon person. Read aloud 1 Corinthians 3:16 and 2 Corinthians 6:16.

Balloon Person Example

2. *Newspaper temples*— (You'll need masking tape and a large stack of newspapers for each group of three or four.) Form groups of three or four by having

30

kids each find two or three other people with the same-color balloon person. Give each group masking tape and a stack of newspapers.

Say: **Use newspapers, tape, and the walls, ceiling, chairs or tables to build a ''temple'' for your group to work inside.**

Just before groups complete their temples, stop them. Have each group get inside its temple. Have group members each share with their group the meaning of the shape they cut out for their name tag.

3. *Dear Gabby*—(For each person you'll need paper and a pencil.) While kids are still inside their temples, read aloud the ''Dear Gabby'' letter. Ask:

Have you felt like the person who wrote this letter? Explain.

Say: **Almost everyone feels like the person who wrote this letter at some time in life. That's because we're all temples under construction. Just like your group's temple, God isn't finished building you yet. Some of his most important construction work on you happens in junior and senior high.**

''Dear Gabby''

Dear *Gabby,*

I've got a terrible problem. I hope you can help me. Lately it seems everything has gone wrong. I used to like the way I looked and was happy with my friends. But all that has changed.

My mom says I'm growing up, but it seems like I'm only getting worse. I get zits on my face at all the wrong times. I say stupid things in front of girls I'd like to get to know. I'm clumsy and weak and can't seem to play any sports. People make fun of me for the smallest things. I feel so alone sometimes. I think things are hopeless for me. Do you have any suggestions?

Signed,

Klutz

Give each person paper and a pencil. Ask kids each to write a letter to "Gabby" that's similar to the one you just read. The letters should express concerns kids have about themselves. Have kids each sign their letter with a creative, made-up name. Then have them each fold their paper once, sign their made-up name again, then fold the paper again. Have kids pile their letters outside their temples.

Collect the piles—keep them separate and note which pile belongs to which group. Tell kids you'll use the letters later in the meeting.

4. *Food, food, food!*—(For each person you'll need a "Food, Food, Food!" handout and a pencil. You'll also need masking tape.) Gather everyone together. Say: **For a moment, think of God as a building contractor. Think of yourself as one of his construction workers. The project you're working on is complex, exciting and important—it's you! There are many ways you can either help or hinder this construction project. One of the best ways to help is to eat properly.**

Give kids each a "Food, Food, Food!" handout and a pencil and have them each fill one out. Have everyone stand in a group in front of you. Tell kids to imagine a line extending from the wall on your left to the wall on your right. The line is a continuum. The wall on your left represents "Very Often" and the wall on your right represents "Hardly Ever."

Say: **As I call out categories of food listed on your handout, stand at the point on the line that best represents your answer. For example, if you eat something sweet once a day, you might stand toward the middle of the line. But if you eat sweets three times a day, you might stand closer to the "Very Often" side of the line.**

After you've gone through the list, say: **A basic, balanced diet each day should include four servings of fruit or vegetables, four servings of bread or cereal, four servings of dairy products and two servings of meat or other high-protein foods.**

Ask kids each to draw a window on the back of their handout. Have them each write one thing inside the window they can do to make their diet more nutritional. Then have them each tape their window on their group's temple.

32

Food, Food, Food!

Instructions: Place an "X" on the continuum after each item to reflect your answer.

How often do you eat or drink these items:

	hardly ever	very often
● sweets		
● whole grain bread, cereal or rice		
● fried foods		
● fruit		
● fast food		
● green vegetables		
● fish		
● red meat		
● sugar-sweetened soft drinks		
● poultry		
● water		
● juice		

Mark a plus (+) by those things that should be a regular part of your diet and mark a minus (-) by those things that shouldn't.

5. *"I'm too fat (skinny)!"*—(You'll need two sheets of newsprint, tape, a marker and an optional weight chart. For each person you'll need a piece of paper and a pencil.) Post the weight chart if you've decided to use one. Tape two sheets of newsprint on a wall. Write "Lose Weight" at the top of one and "Gain Weight" at the top of the other. Draw a line down the center of each sheet and on each, write "Effective" on the left side and "Ineffective" on the right side.

Ask kids to call out effective and ineffective ways to lose or gain weight. Record their answers appropriately on the newsprint.

Say: **Many people in our society are obsessed with either gaining or losing weight. Many of these people are already at their proper weight, but society still convinces them they're too fat or too skinny. Strict dieting is not the best way to lose weight. Proper exercise and a balanced diet are the best ways. Crash dieting can actually make it harder to lose weight because it slows down the rate at which you burn fat.**

And it's a mistake to use steroids to gain weight. Steroids can ruin your health and make you irritable and violent.

Give each person a piece of paper and a pencil. Read aloud 1 John 2:15-17. Say: **Sometimes we listen to society's advice more than God's advice. On your paper, draw a window and write one godly way you can manage your weight. Then tape your window on your group's temple.**

6. *"Am I normal?"*—(For each person you'll need an "Am I Normal?" handout and a pencil.) Give kids each an "Am I Normal?" handout and a pencil. Say: **This is a list of things that may happen while your temple is under construction. Put a checkmark by those things you think are a normal part of growing. Circle those things you think are not normal. And draw a star beside those things you're currently experiencing. You won't be asked to talk about those things you put a star beside.**

After kids finish, choose several items from the list and ask kids if they think each item is normal.

Say: **Everything on the list is a normal part of growing up. Rapid growth, physical changes and growing awareness of sex can create some confusion and embarrassment about your body. Turn your handout over, draw a window, and write one thing you learned in the meeting so**

34

"Am I Normal?"

Instructions: Put a checkmark by those things you think are normal, circle those things that are not normal, and put a star beside those things you are currently experiencing.

- I sometimes feel energetic, other times I feel too lazy to do anything.

- I seem clumsier than I used to be.

- I often worry about the changes I see and feel in my body.

- I eat more than most adults.

- I think about the opposite sex more than I used to.

- I have many unanswered questions about sexuality.

- I get embarrassed easily.

- I don't usually like the way I look.

- I worry about being lazy.

- I have sexual feelings I feel guilty about.

far. Then tape your window on your group's temple.

7. *What society says*—(For each group you'll need two sheets of newsprint, some magazines, tape or glue, and scissors.) Have groups each sit in or near their temple. Give each group the listed materials, and ask groups to title the two newsprints: "Society says I should be worried about . . ." and "Society says I'd be more attractive if I . . ."

Say: **Cut out pictures and words from the magazines that finish the sentence at the top of each newsprint. Tape or glue them to the appropriate newsprint. When you use a picture of a person, cut off a portion of that person before you glue him or her to your newsprint.**

When groups are finished, ask a representative from each one to talk about his or her group's collages.

Read aloud 1 Corinthians 3:10-23 and ask:

If you substituted "God says . . ." for "Society says . . ." on your newsprints, what pictures would you have used instead? Explain.

Say: **Though society says physical perfection, success and material wealth are important, God looks for compassion, honesty, patience, love and humility. The reason I asked you to cut off a piece of each person on your collages is that we're all unfinished. Even the people in the pictures are under construction as far as God is concerned. And he loves us just as we are.**

8. *You're okay*—(You'll need the stacks of "Dear Gabby" letters from activity #3, and for each person you'll need a pencil.) Give each group another group's stack of "Dear Gabby" letters. Have kids each write a reply to one letter using the information they've learned in the meeting. Then have them each fold the letter.

Collect the stacks and return them to the original groups. Have kids each find their letter and read the response.

Have kids form a circle. Close by having kids each pray for the unknown person they wrote a "Dear Gabby" response to. Then celebrate with "temple building" snacks.

Section Two:

FRIENDSHIP

5 Friends: Help or Hindrance?

By Kevin Miller

Few things are more precious to junior highers than their friends. Even if young people realize what bad influences some of their friends are, it's difficult to get them to drop those relationships. The friendship is often too important.

The qualities kids look for in good friends are loyalty and common interests. In kids' minds, friends who're into destructive behavior aren't necessarily bad friends—as long as they're loyal. So kids who abuse drugs together may consider themselves great friends. Most kids won't drop a friend unless they see a better alternative. That's why your junior high group is so important—it can offer kids with bad friends a chance to change.

Use this meeting to help kids evaluate their friendships and make decisions to move toward true friends, including Jesus.

OBJECTIVES

Participants will:

● run a race to see that some friends help move them forward while others hold them back;

● play a flashlight game and discuss biblical friendships to identify what makes a friendship harmful or helpful;

● evaluate their current friendships;

● offer and receive suggestions on how to get out of harmful friendships and establish healthy ones; and

● each take one action to find or strengthen helpful friendships.

BEFORE THE MEETING

Read the meeting, collect supplies and photocopy handouts.

Ask each young person to bring a flashlight. Bring extra flashlights for those who forget.

Buy or make a name tag for each person to pin on. On the back of each one, write one element of the following "trios": Water, Steam, Ice; Moe, Curly, Larry; Red, White, Blue; Burger, Fries, Drink; Dorothy, Blanche, Rose; Tinman, Cowardly Lion, Scarecrow; and Father, Son, Holy Spirit.

Prepare and bring to the meeting a Friendly Refreshment for activity #4—cookies and milk, cheese and crackers, or peanut butter and jelly squares. Bring a recording of friendship music such as Michael W. Smith's "Friends" or Amy Grant's "Sharayah."

Pray for God to help kids get out of bad friendships.

Clear furniture from all or most of the room and make sure windows and other sources of light can be darkened.

THE MEETING

1. *Friendship-trio name tags*—(You'll need a marker and, for each person, a pin and a name tag with the name of a famous trio member printed on the back.) As kids arrive, give each a name tag, marker and pin. Have kids each write their name on the name tag and pin it on.

Say: **Each of you has the name of someone or something in a famous trio written on the back of your name tag. Find the people with the two other names or words that make up your famous trio and sit together.**

If the number of kids participating is not divisible by three, fill up any partial trios with adult leaders.

Say: **This meeting is about friends who work great together, such as Moe, Curly and Larry or the colors red, white and blue. But we'll also talk about friends who don't go together well, such as drinking, drugs and driv-**

ing; oil, water and syrup; or ice cream, hot fudge and
pickles.

  2. *Friendship relay*—(You'll need several pillows or sweat
shirts, and a stopwatch. For each person, you'll need a bandanna
and a flashlight.) Set up the boundaries for a figure-eight racecourse using soft objects such as pillows or sweat shirts. Have
each Friendship Trio be a relay team. Have each team designate
one member as the Rider and the other two as the Carriers. Have
the Carriers get on all fours side by side, facing the same direction. Tie one Carrier's left wrist and ankle to the other Carrier's
right wrist and ankle with bandannas. The Rider will sit on top
of the Carriers as they race the figure-eight course.
  Have kids turn their flashlights on. Turn off the lights. Say:
**The object of this race is for each team's Rider to spur his
or her Carriers through the racecourse from start to finish. The team with the lowest time wins.**
  Pick one team to go first. Tell the rest of the teams to shine
light on the course by turning their flashlights on and off quickly, for a strobe-light effect. Time how long each team takes to
run the course, then give the members of the fastest team each a
bandanna to remind them of their friendship "ties."
  Have kids sit in a circle and shine their flashlights on the
ceiling. Ask the team that had the slowest time:
  ● **What was hardest about trying to run together?**
  Ask the winning team:
  ● **What was the secret of your success?**
  Say: **Just as some teams were slowed because they
struggled to help each other move forward, our own
growth can be slowed by friends who hold us back. Some
friends do move us forward—they help us grow as Christian people. But some friends only weigh us down as we
try to grow in Christ. Lets look at the differences between
a helping-forward friend and a holding-back friend.**

  3. *Famous friends*—(For each Friendship Trio you'll need
a "Famous Friends" handout and a pencil.) Have kids get in their
Friendship Trios again and face the longest wall in the room.
Designate one end of the wall "Helping Forward" and the other
end "Holding Back." Give each Friendship Trio a "Famous
Friends" handout and a pencil. Have each trio study the biblical
friendships and answer the questions. When everyone is finished,
go through each famous friendship and have kids vote on wheth-

40

Famous Friends

Instructions: Read the Bible verses, and then think about each friendship. What makes it good? not so good?

1 Samuel 16:21-23; 18:6-12 David and Saul "Helping forward" qualities in friendship: "Holding back" qualities in friendship:	**1 Samuel 19:1-7; 20:17, 42** David and Jonathan "Helping forward" qualities in friendship: "Holding back" qualities in friendship:
Matthew 14:25-31; 16:13-23 Jesus and Peter "Helping forward" qualities in friendship: "Holding back" qualities in friendship:	**Acts 9:19-21, 26, 27; 15:36-40;** **Galatians 2:11-13** Paul and Barnabas "Helping forward" qualities in friendship: "Holding back" qualities in friendship:

er that friendship is a helping-forward or a holding-back relationship. Each team votes by shining a flashlight beam at a point on the wall. After each vote, ask kids why they chose their answers.

4. *Friendly refreshments*—(You'll need Friendly Refreshments prepared in advance, and cassette tapes or records of friendship music.) Serve the snack and play songs about friendship in the background.

5. *Friendship checkup*—(You'll need a "Friendship Checkup" handout and a pencil for each person.) Form a circle and ask one person to summarize the qualities of a helping-forward friend. Ask another person to summarize the characteristics of a holding-back friend. Distribute the "Friendship Checkup" handouts and pencils.

Say: **You each have a "Friendship Checkup" handout. Choose two of your friends and write their names at the top of your sheet. Now read each statement and checkmark the box after each one that applies. Leave the box blank if the statement doesn't apply.**

Circulate to answer any questions, and make sure kids sit a few feet apart for privacy.

Say: **Now answer some questions silently, to yourself.** Ask:

● **How many boxes did you check for each friend?**

● **How do you feel about the number of boxes you checked?**

● **Do you see problems in either one of your friendships?**

Say: **If you checked very few boxes, be glad for good friendships. If you checked many boxes, realize your friends may be holding you back from becoming all God wants you to be. It's not easy to think that a friend may be hurting you. But if you're in that situation, don't despair. In the time we have left we're going to explore ways to strengthen good friendships and change bad ones.**

6. *Ask the experts*—(You'll need newsprint, a marker and masking tape.) Place three chairs in front of the group and ask for volunteers to sit in them. Say: **These three people represent a panel of experts. I'll read a letter from a person with a friendship problem, and the panel of experts will give that person advice on how to solve that problem. Af-**

42

Friendship Checkup

Instructions: Write the names of two people you'd call friends. Then read the list of statements and checkmark any that describe those friends.

My friend . . .	Friend 1	Friend 2
puts me or other people down a lot.	☐	☐
sometimes "borrows" other people's homework, shoplifts or lies—and pushes me to do it too.	☐	☐
demands all my time.	☐	☐
gets jealous if I hang around anybody else.	☐	☐
makes fun of my going to church or youth group.	☐	☐
won't listen when I say I don't want to do something.	☐	☐
tells other people I did things that I didn't do.	☐	☐
tells dirty jokes to me.	☐	☐
gets me in trouble in class.	☐	☐
calls me names that hurt.	☐	☐
doesn't understand or care about my Christian faith.	☐	☐
makes fun of me if I don't want to do what he or she says.	☐	☐
takes what I told him or her privately and tells it to other people.	☐	☐
tries to get me to do things I'd feel guilty or bad about.	☐	☐

Ask the Experts

Letter #1

Dear Experts:

I've had it with my friend! She puts me down all the time. She thinks she is so cool, but she's the most self-centered person I've ever met. I don't want to be her friend anymore, but if I start hanging around with other people, I know she's going to talk about me. Also, if she asks me why I'm not doing things with her anymore, I don't know what I'd say to her. What should I do?

Letter #2

Dear Experts:

I just moved to my school a few months ago, and most of the kids are snobs. It's been tough finding really good friends. I've started hanging around with two kids at the 7-Eleven, and sometimes they get me doing things I could get in trouble for, such as shoplifting from the store or spray-painting mailboxes. I don't like that, but at least they talk to me and we can joke around together. And if I don't hang around with them, who am I going to be friends with? What should I do?

Letter #3

Dear Experts:

There's this person I like. She's really nice and friendly, and she doesn't put people down a lot. I think we could be good friends. But she already has a lot of friends. How can I become friends with her?

---

ter each letter, we'll switch panel members. And if you're not on the panel, but you have some good advice, raise your hand and let us hear it.

Read each letter from the "Ask the Experts" box and ask the panel members to respond. Once they've responded, open it up to the rest of the group. When you've read all the letters, ask kids to call out principles for (1) getting out of holding-back friendships and (2) starting helping-forward friendships. Write the principles on newsprint and tape it on the wall.

7. *Taking the first step*—(You'll need paper and a pencil for each person.) Distribute paper and pencils. Say: **If your**

44

friends are the helping-forward kind, think of one way you can make those friendships even stronger and write it on your paper. For example, how about giving that friend a gift just for being a good friend? If your friends are the holding-back kind, write one way you can change the situation. If talking to the person is the solution, write the person's name and what you need to say. If you can't think of a way to change the situation, think of one person you'd like to become better friends with and write one way you can make that happen. For example, invite the person to your house for dinner.

Have group members line up side by side and put their arms around each other. Then have the person on one end start curling the line into a ball by rolling it toward the other end. When everyone is wrapped in a circle, squeeze. Thank God for helping-forward friends, and ask him for courage to step away from holding-back friends.

6 Please Like Me

Many junior highers have an almost desperate need to be liked by someone. A best friend becomes vital. Often, best friends are carbon copies of one another—mimicking each other's clothes, speech, mannerisms, even attitudes and values.

Use this meeting to guide your junior highers in handling—in positive, constructive ways—their desire to be liked. It can help you encourage your junior highers to look for positive rather than negative ways to seek others' acceptance.

OBJECTIVES

Participants will:
- evaluate what they do in order to be liked;
- look at types of people who want to be liked;
- discover how others' efforts to be liked influence them;
- discuss what is involved in being liked by others; and
- summarize ideas concerning the need to be liked.

BEFORE THE MEETING

Read the meeting, collect supplies and photocopy handouts. Prepare masks for activity #2.

Invite three to five older teenagers to serve on the panel for activity #5.

46

THE MEETING

1. *Like-a-lot poll*—(You'll need a "Like-a-Lot Poll" handout and a pencil for each person.) To start kids thinking about being liked, give arriving kids each a "Like-a-Lot Poll" handout and a pencil. Tell them to complete the poll as quickly as possible. When kids are done, collect the polls. Ask a sponsor to tally them while kids do the next activity.

2. *Like-me masks*—(You'll need a mask for each person. See the "Like-Me Masks" box for directions on making masks.) Explain that we often wear masks to get others to like us. As you tie masks on junior highers, make sure kids each see only the back of their own mask. Tell them to try to guess what type of person they are, based on what other kids say to them. Instruct others to say the phrases on the front of each mask. Be careful not to place a mask on a kid who has similar characteristics. For example, don't tie Joe Jock's mask on a football player.

After several minutes, let kids remove the masks and place them on the floor where they can be seen. Ask kids each to share how they felt wearing the mask.

Ask:

● **Did others like you? How could you tell?**

● **What does each mask-person do to be liked?** (For example, Rich Richard may offer to buy people things. Wilma Wallflower wants to be liked, but doesn't know how.)

● **Which types of kids are most liked at your school? at your church? by your friends? Why?**

● **What other masks do kids wear in order to be liked by others?**

3. *Like-me letters*—(You'll need five or six objects that have different textures. For example: rough sandpaper, a lumpy beanbag, sticky candy, a smooth mirror, a furry fabric.) Explain that sometimes we use "texture talk" to express how we feel about others. We might say: "He rubs me the wrong way"; "She sticks to me like glue"; "Our relationship is as smooth as glass"; "He's like a warm fuzzy." As you talk, pass around objects that have different textures.

Place each object in a different part of the room. Instruct kids to go to the object that best describes how they'd feel about the person who wrote each letter you're about to read. Read aloud each letter in the "Like-Me Letters" box; pause after each

47

Like-a-Lot Poll

Instructions: Check all you would do.

In order to be liked, I would:

(1) give answers to a friend on a homework assignment. _____

(2) smile even when I don't feel happy. _____

(3) cuss because it's cool. _____

(4) turn in an assignment on time to please a teacher. _____

(5) steal a magazine for a friend. _____

(6) compliment someone I don't hang around with. _____

(7) smoke because my friends do. _____

(8) earn good grades to please my parents. _____

(9) buy brand-name clothes because others wear them. _____

(10) help with a mission project because I promised I would. _____

(11) do anything to get a date. _____

(12) keep my body and clothes clean and neat. _____

(13) lie to my parents in order to go with friends to a concert. _____

(14) keep my room clean to help my mom. _____

(15) ask my parents to buy me the latest electronic fad. _____

(16) invite a new neighbor to my party. _____

(17) hang out every Saturday at a mall. _____

(18) write thank-you notes for gifts. _____

(19) loan money to everyone who wants it. _____

(20) earn money, so I won't have to borrow from parents or friends. _____

Total the checks by the odd numbers: _____.

Total the checks by the even numbers: _____.

If more *odd* numbers are checked, beware! You're in danger of being controlled by others. Your actions may leave you with shallow friendships.

If more *even* numbers are checked, hooray! Your healthy actions may bring lasting friendships. In fact, you can influence others in a positive way.

48

Like-Me Masks

Instructions: Prepare masks from paper plates and string. Cut out holes for eyes. Tie a string to both sides of the plate. On the front of each plate write the name of a stereotypical kid, such as the following. Also, write two or more comments others would make to this person. Make up additional names and comments, as appropriate to your area.

Joe Jock—Hey dude, what's the score?/How's your backhand?

Cindy Cheerleader—Oh, I just love your smile./You have so much enthusiasm.

Tommy Tuneful—You're so talented./I wish I could play the guitar like you.

Wilma Wallflower—Don't you get lonely standing off by yourself?/How come you never talk to anyone?

Rich Richard—Can I borrow a dollar?/What have you bought lately?

Shy Susie—Hold your head up!/Why do you blush when anyone talks to you?

Steve Stud—Who's your date this week?/Where's the action, man?

Party Patty—Where's the party?/Wow, you're really loaded tonight!

Smart Sam—Can you help me with my algebra?/I heard you aced the exam.

Punk Paula—Love your hair!/Aren't those bracelets heavy?

one to let kids move to an object. After each letter is read, ask:
- **Why did you choose that texture?**
- **What makes you like or dislike this person?**
- **How does this person try to gain acceptance?**

Report the "Like-a-Lot Poll" results. Evaluate by asking:
- **What do most of you do to get others to like you?**
- **What actions that others are willing to do to be liked surprise you?**
- **How do others pressure you to do things so they'll like you?**
- **What actions done to be liked are not acceptable?**
- **What actions are acceptable?**

4. *Being liked advice #1*—(You'll need the four teams' scripture references written on slips of paper, four Bibles, pencils and paper.) Explain that you have some advice on how to be

Like-Me Letters

Dear Friend:

I looked everywhere for you, but couldn't find you. That's okay. I'll talk to you tomorrow. You can always find me waiting by your locker in the morning and between classes. I enjoy sitting with you at lunch when your so-called friends will let me. Until I see you again—

Carol

Dear Friend:

No one likes me. I never wear the right clothes or fix my hair just right. I try to be friendly, but everyone ignores me. Maybe it's because I'm not very smart. I guess people just don't understand me.

Harry

Dear Friend:

Hey! I just thought we'd have a good time cruising around. You didn't have to get so mad when that guy pulled the booze out from under his seat. A few sips isn't a big deal. Don't be so uptight next time!

Pat

Dear Friend:

I'm sorry you're grounded. I'll try to call every day and let you know what's happening. Maybe your folks will let you go out next week, if you act "normal" (according to parents). Hang in there!

Frieda

liked by others. Form four teams. Give each team a Bible, a slip of paper with scripture references written on it, pencils and paper. Tell teams each to determine what their verses say about liking yourself or being liked by others. Have teams write each verse in modern-day words to share with the large group.

- Team 1—Proverbs 3:7; 12:3; and 22:1
- Team 2—Proverbs 3:5; 12:15; and 12:26
- Team 3—Proverbs 13:20; 16:7; and 23:7a
- Team 4—Proverbs 10:9; and 22:24-25

Let each team read its rewritten, modern-day proverbs. Explain that Proverbs gives excellent advice on how to be liked by parents, friends, neighbors and others.

5. *Being liked advice #2*—Have a panel of three to five older kids (high school juniors, seniors or college-age young people) suggest ways to be liked. Encourage questions from junior highers.

6. *Like-me proverbs*—(You'll need pencils and paper for kids.) Help kids sort through the ideas in this meeting. Give each group member a piece of paper and a pencil. Form the same teams used in activity #4. Tell teams each to write two proverbs based on the advice they've heard. Have kids share these proverbs.

7. *Like-me-please coupons*—(You'll need a "Like-Me-Please Coupon" and a pencil for each person.) Help kids each choose one positive idea to use in getting others to like them. Hand out the "Like-Me-Please Coupons."

Instruct kids each to fill out a coupon with one thing to do to be liked by someone. For example, a coupon to Mom might say, "I will wash the dishes for a week." Or a coupon to a friend might say, "I will help you with your algebra homework for two weeks." Suggest kids adapt the Bible Proverbs or advice from the panel, or create ideas for the coupon. Close by letting kids tell about their coupons and deliver them (if the people they're for are in the room).

Like-Me Please Coupon

Instructions: Choose a person you want to grow closer to and fill out this coupon with one thing you will do to help that person like you.

TO:

FROM:

To help you like me more, I will_____

for _____ .

Special Series: *By Ann Cannon*

Coping With Peer Pressure

The right amount of rain in the right place at the right time is good. We'd have no crops without it. But too much rain in the wrong place at the wrong time can destroy.

Peer pressure is the same way.

A little positive peer pressure at youth group meetings can help your junior highers stay on the sometimes difficult path that leads to God. But outside church walls, kids often face a raging torrent of negative peer pressure. Sometimes they're overwhelmed by the flood.

According to a TEENAGE Magazine reader survey, 80 percent of young people give in to peer pressure at least once a week, and 60 percent admit they pressure others. Peer pressure ranked second in a Group Publishing survey of problems parents say they face with their kids.

Junior highers are at an uncertain, vulnerable age. They look to friends for the intimacy, acceptance and care that once came from their families. Though kids say they want independence, their actions show they're dependent on others for determining values.

HOW TO USE THIS SERIES

1. Carefully read the entire series. Have a Bible handy to read scripture verses when they're given. Adapt the activities to your junior highers' maturity and personalities.

2. Focus on the benefits of positive peer pressure, rather than sermonizing on the evils of negative peer pressure. Kids know succumbing to negative peer pressure is wrong; but they're looking for positive alternatives. Follow up the series with a lock-in or retreat. This will give you a chance to develop a positive, accepting environment for kids.

1 *The Truth About Peer Pressure* (Meeting #1)

*T*oday's kids live in a world that exposes them to more violence and explicit sex through the media than ever before. They have less contact with families, have more available knowledge due to increased technology, and feel increasing social pressures to make adult decisions.

These social forces leave kids vulnerable to the shifting whims of their peer groups. Kids desperately want to be accepted—to fit in. That's why fads can travel so quickly through the teenage subculture, then die out as fast as they started.

Use this meeting to help kids discover how peer pressure happens and why they're susceptible to it.

OBJECTIVES

Participants will:
- define peer pressure;
- identify the subtle and obvious influences of friends;
- see how peer pressure affects others; and
- learn one way to counteract peer pressure.

BEFORE THE MEETING

Read the meeting and "How to Use This Series" (page 51). Also read the entire three-part series before doing this first meeting. Collect supplies and photocopy handouts.

Ask an adult volunteer to be ready to write the top three choices in each category for the Peer Poll in activity #1.

Write "Get every person on your team to say no to you" on each of two 3×5 cards for activity #5. Then print on the other side of each card "Just Say No Instruction Card."

THE MEETING

1. Peer poll—(You'll need a "Peer Poll" handout and a pencil for each person.) As kids arrive, give them each a "Peer Poll" handout and a pencil. Have them each complete the poll without comparing answers. Collect the polls, and have an adult volunteer tally the results to find the top three choices in each category. Tell kids they'll find out the poll results later in the meeting.

2. Brand name bonanza—(You'll need a Coke. For each person you'll need a "Brand Name Bonanza" handout and a pencil.) Give each person a "Brand Name Bonanza" handout.

Say: **This game's goal is to find people who use, wear or enjoy the same things you do. Look at your "Brand Name Bonanza" handout. Mingle and find people who fit the categories; then ask them each to write their name in the appropriate squares. To win, you need to have four squares in a row—up and down, across or diagonally—signed by other people. The winner will receive the #1-selling soft drink in the world—Coke.**

After the winner is rewarded, have kids sit in a circle. Ask:

● **What is peer pressure?**

● **Is it positive or negative? Explain.**

● **Why did you find so many similarities in what others use, wear or enjoy?**

● **How do your friends influence what you buy and what you do?**

3. Pressure points—(You'll need four Bibles and the 17 Pressure Points cut out from the "Pressure Points" box. For each person you'll need construction paper, markers and scissors.) Write "ME" on a circle of construction paper and place it on the

54

Peer Poll

Instructions: Write a response to each statement.

Name a current movie you like. _____

Name an activity you like to do with friends. _____

Name your favorite brand of jeans. _____

Name your favorite school subject. _____

Name a common item of clothing for fashion-conscious junior highers. _____

Name a place where you like to hang out. _____

Name your least favorite school subject. _____

Name a fear you have. _____

Name something you do because your friends do it. _____

Name a person you admire. _____

Brand Name Bonanza

Instructions: Find people who fit the categories below and ask them to sign the box that applies to them. To win, you must get four signatures in a row—either vertically, across or diagonally. Find someone:

who uses the same toothpaste as you.	who uses the same soap as you.	who ate at the same place you last ate.	who wears the same brand of watch as you.
whose favorite song is the same as yours.	who saw the same movie you last saw.	who watches your favorite TV program.	who's wearing the same brand of jeans or pants you're wearing.
who's wearing the same brand of shoes you're wearing.	whose favorite clothing store is the same as yours.	whose favorite sport is the same as yours.	whose favorite food is the same as yours.
who pays the same amount as you for a haircut.	whose favorite TV actor or actress is the same as yours.	who went to the same party you last went to.	who's wearing the same brand shirt or sweat shirt you're wearing.

56

Pressure Points

Instructions: Cut apart these strips and give one to each young person.

1. Being independent from family	10. Media influence
2. Parents divorcing or separating	11. Fearing rejection
3. Desiring to be popular	12. Desiring to be grown up
4. Needing to fit in	13. Looking for temporary pleasures
5. Money problems within family	14. Having poor self-esteem
6. High expectations from parents	15. Trying to escape reality
7. Moving to a new place	16. Not having enough parental influence
8. Rebellion against authority	17. Having too much parental influence
9. Fearing being different	

floor in the middle of your group. Give each person construction paper, a marker, scissors and a Pressure Point. (If you have fewer than 17 kids, give more than one Pressure Point to some. If you have more than 17 kids, form pairs or teams.)

Say: **Draw and then cut out a large arrow from your construction paper. Decorate your arrow, and write your Pressure Point on it.**

Ask each person:

● **Is the Pressure Point you've written on your arrow positive or negative? Explain.**

● **How might that Pressure Point increase peer pressure?**

As kids finish answering the questions, have them each place their arrows on the floor, pointing to the ME construction paper circle.

Say: **Peer pressure is nothing new. People in the Bible had to deal with it all the time.**

Form four groups and give each group a Bible. Assign each group one of the following scripture passages:

● Judges 2:11-19   ● 1 Samuel 8:4-7, 19-20
● Matthew 26:69-75   ● Luke 17:11-19

Say: **Read aloud your scripture passage; then as a group decide who gave in to peer pressure. Cut out a construction paper circle and write that person's name on it. Then decide what kinds of peer pressure were involved in the situation. (Look at the Pressure Points arrows for ideas.) For each pressure, cut out an arrow and write the pressure on it. Arrange your arrows and circles on the floor as before.**

Have groups each talk about their display. Then form a circle and ask:

● **What modern-day situation is similar to what happened in your scripture passage?**

● **How do you know if your friends are pressuring you to do something right? something wrong?**

● **Who has the most influence over your choices right now? Explain.**

4. Friendly feud—(You'll need the Peer Poll results—the top three picks in each category—and a score sheet.) Form two teams. Have teams line up single file at one end of the room while you stand at the other end.

Say: **We've written the top three answers to each cate-**

58

gory in the Peer Poll. On "go," the first person in each line will race to me. The first person to touch me wins a chance to give me one of the top three answers to a particular category. If he or she answers correctly, I'll ask the next two people on that person's team to give me the remaining two answers of the top three. For each correct answer, that team will receive 100 points.

If the first person to reach me doesn't give one of the top three answers to the category, the other person who raced to me will have a chance to answer. If he or she answers correctly, I'll ask the next two people on that person's team for the remaining two answers.

After three team members respond to a category, I'll read the top answers. Those three people should go to the back of the team's line. We'll repeat the same steps for all the categories on the Peer Poll. The team with the most points at the end of the game wins.

After you declare a winner, say: **Peer pressure can be harmless when it concerns the way you style your hair. But sometimes peer pressure is used to subtly manipulate you into doing something you really don't want to do— such as getting drunk. It's important to recognize subtle peer pressure and know how to react.**

5. *Just say no*—(You'll need two "Just Say No Instruction Cards," and for each person you'll need a blank 3×5 card.) Have kids stay in the same teams from activity #4. Give one person on each team a "Just Say No Instruction Card." Without letting the group know what's happening, whisper to these two people: On "go," try to be the first person to get all of your team members to say no. Allow two minutes to complete the task.

Form a circle and ask:
● **Is it hard to say no to your friends at times? Why or why not?**
● **How can you say no to a friend without hurting his or her feelings?**

Give each person a blank 3×5 card. Have kids each write one pressure they feel from their friends—either positive or negative. Then have them each write one pressure they can say no to during the next week. Close in prayer. Have kids who wrote positive peer pressures thank God for his help. Have kids who wrote negative peer pressures ask God for help in battling the temptation to give in to the pressure.

8 *From Bad News to Good News* (Meeting #2)

A Scholastic Update study found that pressure to smoke is the #1 peer pressure kids face. So peer pressure is responsible, at least in part, for the #2 killer in our society—cancer.

According to Sharon Scott, author of Peer Pressure Reversal, kids should be taught at an early age how to say no to peer pressure. "Today's youth are experiencing negative peer pressure at a much earlier age than children 15 to 20 years ago," she says, "which just increases the difficulty in their attempts at decision-making. Decision-making needs to be taught—it is not inherent."

Use this meeting to help your junior highers identify negative peer pressure and deal with it positively.

OBJECTIVES

Participants will:
- identify negative types of peer pressure;
- discover the messages that create negative peer pressure;
- examine positive ways to handle peer pressure; and
- learn to see themselves as worthy people, able to handle life's pressures.

60

BEFORE THE MEETING

Read the meeting, collect supplies and photocopy handouts.

Make Peertionary Cards by writing each of the following 15 words on a separate 3×5 card for activity #1: smoking, cussing, lying, hairstyle, clothes, drugs, alcohol, pregnancy, shoplifting, cheating, church, sports, cliques, music, movies.

Write "Steps to Resisting Peer Pressure" at the top of a large sheet of newsprint. Have this newsprint ready for activity #3. Write the following steps for resisting peer pressure on the newsprint:

● Step One: Check out the scene—Ask yourself, "Is this trouble?" You know it's trouble if you'll break a law or make someone in charge mad.

● Step Two: Make a good decision—Think about what could happen; weigh both sides; then make your decision.

● Step Three: Act to avoid trouble.

THE MEETING

1. *Peertionary*—(You'll need masking tape, three or more long sheets of newsprint, three markers, the Peertionary Cards, and for each person you'll need a balloon.) Tape the three sheets of newsprint vertically, side by side, on a wall. (Have more newsprint set aside in case you need it.) Form three teams.

Say: **We're going to play a modified version of the game Pictionary. Our game is called Peertionary. I'll ask a volunteer from each team to come up in turn, grab a marker and draw a picture of a word I'll show them. Each volunteer will have one minute to draw while his or her team tries to guess their word. Each word will be different, and will have something to do with peer pressure. For each word guessed, your team will receive 100 points. The team with the most points at the end of the game wins.**

After each word is guessed, tape the 3×5 card with that word underneath the winning team's picture. Repeat the words until all 15 words are guessed.

After the game, ask kids to vote on which words are the result of negative peer pressure. Circle those words on the newsprint. Ask:

● **Why are these words associated with negative peer pressure?**

● **Are the words not circled associated with positive peer pressure? Why or why not?**

To help kids see how peer pressure affects them, give each one a balloon. Say: **Every time I say something you feel pressured to do, blow a big breath into your balloon.**

Read aloud each type of peer pressure from the Peertionary game, and add extra phrases such as fighting with a family member; laughing at someone who's different from you; avoiding people who aren't in the "in" crowd; and watching R-rated movies.

After you've read all the words, have kids compare the size of their balloons. Ask:

Is anyone's balloon about to pop?

Say: **You can tie off your balloon and keep all that pressure inside, or you can let go of the balloon and release the pressure. It's the same with peer pressure. And in this meeting, we'll discover ways to release negative peer pressure from our lives.**

Have kids let their balloons go and collect the balloons after they land.

Heckler Pressures

"If you're my friend, you'll believe me."
"I dare you."
"It doesn't matter; it's just a game."
"Only little kids play games like this."
"Are you chicken?"

---

2. *Say what?*—(You'll need two copies of the "Heckler Pressures" card. For each person you'll need a blindfold.) Have kids each put on a blindfold. Say: **Your goal is to form a triangle that includes everyone in the group. You may speak to and touch one another, but you can't peek.**

Then take three kids aside and remove their blindfolds.

62

Don't tell the blindfolded kids about the three people you pulled aside. Tell one of the kids to give the blindfolded kids helpful instructions. Tell the other two to heckle and give confusing instructions. Give the latter two kids each a "Heckler Pressures" card. Tell them each to use the card for heckling ideas.

After the blindfolded kids decide they've formed a triangle, have them remove their blindfolds. Tell kids about the three people you pulled aside. Ask:

● **Who did you listen to? Why?**

● **What did you hear that influenced your decisions?**

● **How did listening to the wrong people make your task more difficult?**

● **How did listening to the right people make it easier?**

● **What are some of the phrases people used to pressure you during the task?**

● **How are those phrases used to pressure people in other situations?**

3. *Saying no to peer pressure*—(You'll need the "Steps to Resisting Peer Pressure" newsprint taped on a wall, and masking tape. For each person you'll need a "Saying No Without Losing Your Friends" handout and a pencil. Write each of the following references on separate pieces of paper:

● 1 Kings 18:20-38   ● Esther 2:5, 7, 17
● Esther 4:11-18   ● John 8:3-9
● Romans 12:1-2   ● 1 Corinthians 8:4-13)

Say: **People will pressure you all your life. But you can choose how you'll respond. People in the Bible faced many of the same peer pressures you face today. And you can learn from their experiences.**

Form six or fewer groups. Give each group a paper with a scripture verse on it. Tell each group to read its scripture, then write on its paper one piece of advice—based on that scripture—for fighting peer pressure. Tape the papers on the "Steps to Resisting Peer Pressure" newsprint. Talk about the steps listed on the newsprint, and ask kids how their scriptural advice fits with those steps.

Give each person a "Saying No Without Losing Your Friends" handout.

Say: **Your group should choose one of the peer pressures from the Peertionary activity. Then role play that pressure. Choose one person in your group to role-play**

63

Saying No Without Losing Your Friends

You can avoid peer pressure without turning off your friends by trying one of the following responses:

1. Just say no. Stick with your response.

2. Leave. Walk away confidently. Don't stay around. You'll just get into an argument.

3. Ignore the suggestion. Either pretend you didn't hear your friend or start talking about something else.

4. Make an excuse. Think of something else you could be doing.

5. Change the subject. Pick a topic that interests your friend.

6. Make a joke. Humor lets you say no to the pressure without threatening your friend.

7. Act shocked. Be surprised by what your friend asks you to do.

8. Suggest a better idea. This will give you a way out.

9. Return the challenge. If your friend says, ''If you were really my friend, you'd do it,'' you can say, ''If you were really my friend, you wouldn't ask me to do it.''

Adapted from *How to Say No and Keep Your Friends*, by Sharon Scott, copyright 1986, HRD Press Inc., 22 Amherst Rd., Amherst, MA, 01002—1-800-822-2801. $7.95.

64

the person being pressured. That person should use the "Saying No Without Losing Your Friends" tips for ideas. The rest of your group should try to convince that person to give in to their pressure.

After groups present their role plays, have kids read the "Saying No Without Losing Your Friends" tips and talk about the options listed. Ask:

Which idea is the best for getting out of a pressured situation? Explain.

4. *It's in the bag*—(For each person you'll need a paper bag and a 3×5 card.) Give kids each a paper bag and 3×5 card. Say: **One of the best ways to fight peer pressure is to recognize how special and unique you are. You don't have to do what everyone else is doing, because God didn't make you like everyone else.**

Have kids each write their name and three unique things about themselves on their 3×5 card. For example, suggest they write a favorite place to visit, a favorite activity, food or book, a talent or skill, or a secret desire. Then ask kids each to put the 3×5 card in their bag and pass it to you. Mix up the bags. One by one, open the bags and read the card inside. Challenge kids to guess which person wrote each card. Say: **Even though you're pressured to be the same as everyone else, you're each unique.**

5. *Picture this*—(You'll need a mirror.) Form a circle. Go around the circle holding a mirror in front of each person in turn. As you stand in front of each person, say: **(Name), I appreciate you because . . .**

9 You Can Do It! (Meeting #3)

A typical junior higher on a typical day plays many roles. Student, child, teammate, outcast, friend, foe, rebel, counselor. Peer relationships often determine when kids will drop one role and pick up another. So kids are most vulnerable to peer pressure when they're developing those relationships— in the locker room, at the movies or on the telephone.

Fighting on the peer pressure battlefield can be brutal. And you won't always be around to help your kids "fight the good fight." So use this meeting to help kids learn to fight for themselves when no one else is around.

OBJECTIVES

Participants will:
- experience how others influence their decisions;
- find biblical help for living in today's world;
- learn how to respond to peer pressure by making decisions in case study situations; and
- evaluate how they respond to friends' pressure.

BEFORE THE MEETING

Read the meeting, collect supplies and photocopy handouts.

For activity #1, cut out retail catalog pages with pictures of things junior highers enjoy, such as clothing, albums, food, stereos, jewelry and telephones. Be sure each page gives the price of each item pictured. Gather or make enough play money to give each person $1,000 in an envelope.

THE MEETING

1. *Money talks*—(You'll need pictures of things kids enjoy set out on a table, and for each person you'll need an envelope with $1,000 in play money in it and a pencil.) As kids arrive, give them each a pencil and an envelope with play money in it. Ask them each to write their name in their envelope's upper left corner.

Say: **Look at the pictures on the table. You have 10 minutes to decide which items you'll buy with your money. You must spend all the money in your envelope. To buy an item, simply write its description and cost on the outside of your envelope. Then remove enough money from your envelope to pay for the item and place the money on the table. You may talk with others to help you decide what to buy.**

Have kids hand in their envelopes after 10 minutes. Read what each person decided to purchase, then ask:

● **Were you influenced to buy things that others were buying? Why or why not?**

● **How do your friends influence what you buy in real life?**

● **What are some other areas in which friends influence your decisions?**

2. *Designer clothes*—(You'll need a large sheet of newsprint, construction paper, markers, scissors, tape and the "Team Scriptures" assignment cards from page 67.) Form five or fewer teams. Say: **Each team represents a different clothing, hat or shoe manufacturer—you decide which one. Your job as a team is to design and produce a pair of designer shoes, a dress or shirt, a hat, a pair of pants, or a jacket using the newsprint, construction paper, markers, scissors and tape provided. But instead of the designer label, you'll substitute a key word or phrase from the Bible that offers help in dealing with peer pressure.**

Give teams each a scripture assignment card. Say: **After your team reads its scripture passages, pick someone on your team to be a model. Then, decide on one key phrase**

Team Scriptures

Instructions: Cut apart these assignment cards and give one to each team.

- Team 1—Hebrews 12:1-2 and 1 John 3:15-17; 5:4-5

- Team 2—Philippians 4:8-9; 1 Thessalonians 5:21-22; and 1 Timothy 6:11-12

- Team 3—Galatians 2:20; Philippians 4:13; and 1 Peter 3:15, 17-18; 5:6-9

- Team 4—Colossians 3:1-3, 12-14; 2 Thessalonians 3:3; and James 4:7-8

- Team 5—1 Corinthians 6:19-20; Ephesians 6:10-18; and 1 John 4:4

68

or word that offers advice in dealing with peer pressure. Then use that word or phrase as the "designer label" for the clothing you'll design. For example, instead of a "Members Only" jacket, you might design a "God is with me" jacket. Instead of Reebok shoes, you could design "Perseverance" shoes. When you're finished, have your team's model display your creation.

As kids model their clothing, point out the key words or phrases. Ask teams each to explain why they chose a certain word or phrase.

3. *Peer pressure land*—(You'll need the "Case Study Game Cards.") Make a game board by laying the "Case Study Game Cards" in sequence on the floor in a winding route. Form three teams.

Say: **Now that we've discovered some peer pressure advice from the Bible, let's apply it by playing Peer Pressure Land. Each team should appoint one person to move around the game board. This person won't be allowed to answer the questions.**

Here's how you'll play. Your game-piece person will read aloud the case study card, and your team must decide on a response to what is read by choosing one of two answers. After you've chosen an answer, have the game-piece person look on the back of the card to determine how many spaces to move backward or forward. All three teams will choose their answers in turn, and all three game pieces will move in turn. The team that has moved farthest along the game board at the end of the game wins.

Have the game-piece people begin by reading aloud the first case study card (0—A). Then have them each ask their team for an answer and move the appropriate number of spaces forward or backward.

4. *Taking your temperature*—(For each person you'll need a "Peer Pressure Thermometer" handout and a marker.) Say: **Most people give in to peer pressure because they don't feel confident or good about themselves. If you feel good about yourself, you won't be easily influenced by the negative things others want you to do.**

Give each person a "Peer Pressure Thermometer" handout and a marker. Ask kids each to read the statements from bottom

Case Study Game Cards

Instructions: Cut apart each of the game cards as indicated and fold it along the ''fold'' line so that the writing shows. Tape the two sides together using clear tape.

Front side	Back side
Card 0—A An older friend asks you to go to the movie on a Friday night. You decide to: (A) go with your friend; or (B) invite your friend over to watch a new video.	**Card 0—B** If you chose A, it sounds like a good idea. Move ahead five spaces. If you chose B, it sounds like a good idea. Move ahead four spaces.
Card 1—A Your folks come home early and interrupt your passionate embraces. What do you say to your parents? What do you say to your friend?	**Card 1—B** After answering, move ahead one space and stay there. The End.
Card 2—A The usher sees you are underage. He tells you to leave the theater. What do you say to your parents when you call them to come pick you up?	**Card 2—B** After answering, move ahead one space and stay there. The End.
Card 3—A The video gets really scary. You cling to your friend. Things quickly lead to heavy kisses. You: (A) decide you're still in control, and besides, it feels natural; or (B) turn on the lights, make a joke, and go to the kitchen to make popcorn.	**Card 3—B** If you chose A, things move quickly beyond just kisses. Go back two spaces. If you chose B, this gives you time to think. Move ahead five spaces.

Fold Line

continued

Card 4—A

Your friend is an older guy, and you're a young gal. On the night he comes over, your parents have already gone to a party. You:

(A) suggest going to the movies after all; or

(B) stay home since you've rented a video.

Card 4—B

If you chose A, it sounds like a good idea. Move ahead one space.

If you chose B, he turns down the lights and turns on the scary video. Go back one space.

Card 5—A

At the movie, you buy tickets for a PG movie, but once inside your friend challenges you to go to the R-rated movie that's playing in the same theater. You're underage, but your friend is not. You:

(A) try to talk your friend out of going to the R-rated movie; or

(B) go ahead to the R-rated movie since you've heard it's really good, and the rating is undeserved.

Card 5—B

If you chose A, at least you're trying. Move ahead two spaces.

If you chose B, you get carded by an usher. Go back three spaces.

Fold Line

Card 6—A

An older kid sees you in the movie. She doesn't like you, so she reports you to an usher. The usher tells you to leave the theater. What do you say to your parents when you call them to pick you up?

Card 6—B

After answering, move ahead one space and stay there.
The End.

Card 7—A

Your friend won't be talked out of the idea of attending the R-rated movie. Your friend calls you a sissy and goes to the R-rated movie. You:

(A) follow, hoping to change his or her mind; or

(B) go into the PG movie.

Card 7—B

If you chose A, you're now in the R-rated movie illegally. Go back one space.

If you chose B, you are now in the movie you planned to see. Move ahead two spaces.

continued

✂ -

Card 8—A

Your friend calls you a cheap flirt. What do you say?

Card 8—B

After answering, move ahead three spaces and stay there.
The End.

Card 9—A

Your friend won't take you home and says you're a wimp. What do you say to your parents when you call them to pick you up?

Fold Line

Card 9—B

After answering, move ahead one space and stay there.
The End.

Card 10—A

Congratulations! You made wise choices!

to top and stop when they reach a statement that's *not true* for them. Then have them each color in the thermometer up to that statement.

Say: **The higher you marked your temperature, the more likely you are to rely on others for approval. And that makes you more vulnerable to peer pressure.**

Read aloud Psalm 100. Ask:

● **If these words are true—that God has made each of us—how does that affect the way you see yourself?**

● **Whose opinion about you is really more important— God's or your friends'? Explain.**

● **What's one way you'd like to improve who you are?**

5. *Positive pressure*—Form a circle and put one person in the middle. Tell those in the circle to call out things they like about the person in the center. Keep things moving by allowing only two or three comments from each person. Then ask the next person to step into the center. Continue until all group members have been in the center. Close by praying for God's help and strength to fight negative peer pressure.

72

Peer Pressure Thermometer

Instructions: Read these statements from bottom to top and stop when you reach a statement that's *not true* for you. Then color in the thermometer up to that statement.

I'm willing to do anything to be liked —————————

I want friends' approval for my actions—————————

I want everyone to like me —————————————

I want friends' approval for my clothing ——————————

I want my best friends to like me ——————————

I like myself—————————————————

Section Three:

FAMILY

10 Growing Up

By Jeanne Leland and Katie Abercrombie

Adolescence is a time of branching out and learning to be independent. It's a process that begins at birth, and it becomes especially intense during the junior high years. Junior highers want to make their own decisions, develop a personal style and establish values.

Use this meeting to let junior highers talk about fears and joys of branching out from their families. It will help them see the relationship between gaining freedom and accepting responsibility, and how their roots, families and faith can help them become secure and independent.

OBJECTIVES

Participants will:

● express the joys and frustrations they're experiencing as they attempt to branch out from their families;

● look at the relationship between independence and responsibility;

● compare the freedoms and responsibilities they had, have or expect to have at different times of their lives;

● see what God expects as they grow as independent and responsible people;

● discover how their roots help them branch out; and

● determine ways they can bear fruit.

BEFORE THE MEETING

Read the meeting, collect supplies and photocopy handouts. Have several group members bring fruit and fruit punch for refreshments.

Think about some of your struggles in branching out from your family. Be aware of the different definitions of "family" that may be present in your group. Be supportive of kids who may not have strong family values as they attempt to establish positive values.

Place a potted tree (or a branch in a pot) in the center of the room. Tape onto the wall a sheet of newsprint with the following incomplete sentences:

- I bear fruit in my life by . . .
- I know I'm connected to Christ because . . .
- A time I felt cut off from my roots was . . .
- Something I need to do differently to bear more fruit

is . . .

- I know Christ's joy is in me because . . .

THE MEETING

1. *Branching out*—(You'll need masking tape, markers and leaves cut in various shapes from construction paper—for example: maple, sweet gum, oak. Make each leaf type in multiples of three; you'll need one leaf per person.) Give each person a construction paper leaf and a marker. Have kids each write on their leaf:

(1) their name;

(2) one new freedom they've gained recently;

(3) a new responsibility they have; and

(4) an area where they're struggling to be more independent.

Have kids each find two other kids with the same kind of leaf they have and form a group. Have group members each share the four things they wrote on their leaf. When they finish, have them each tape their leaf on the tree in the middle of the room.

2. *New freedoms, new responsibilities*—Say: **In this meeting we're going to talk about becoming more independent. This is a time in your life when you change a lot—you look, act and think differently from when you were a child. Your parents and teachers probably expect**

76

more from you. You want to make your own decisions. You're becoming an adult, and that means accepting more responsibility to gain more independence. Bring your chairs together in a circle. We'll play a game that will help us see what each of us is experiencing in our branching-out journey.

When everyone is sitting in a circle, explain that you'll read aloud some statements. If a person feels a statement is true for him or her, that person should move two seats to the right. If someone feels a statement doesn't apply to him or her, that person should move two seats to the left. If someone is unsure about whether a statement applies to him or her, that person shouldn't move. Kids will end up sitting on each other's laps. Read aloud the "Freedom and Responsibility Statements," allowing the kids a little time to think and move after each one. Pay attention to kids' movements for discussion after the game.

Freedom and Responsibility Statements

1. My parents and I disagree about when I should come home at night.
2. I wish my parents would let me make more of my own decisions.
3. My parents expect me to do too much around the house.
4. Sometimes I feel like a little kid in my family.
5. I think I have too much freedom.
6. I don't like my parents to choose the clothes I buy.
7. Some of my teachers give me so much work that I don't think they know I have other classes.
8. My parents and I argue more now than we used to.
9. I value the same things my parents do.
10. I think I don't do enough to help my family.
11. There are a lot of things that I want to do that my parents won't let me do.
12. My parents and I argue about my room being messy.
13. I have a lot more freedom than I used to have.
14. I like doing my part to help around the house.
15. Sometimes I feel scared about making my own decisions because I might mess up.

Have everyone get comfortable. Discuss how the kids responded to the statements. You'll likely conclude that, in general, young people want more freedom, and parents expect more responsibility. Ask your group members if they agree. Have them comment on anything significant they noticed during the game. Help them understand that the tension they may feel between themselves and their parents is a normal part of growing up—a result of their becoming more independent.

3. *From tiny seedling to great tree*—(You'll need a "From Tiny Seedling to Great Tree" handout and a pencil for each person.) Give each person a handout and a pencil. Form six groups (a group can be one person). Remind kids that we gain freedom and responsibility as we grow up. Have them think about a time in their lives when they had less freedom and responsibility than they do now. Then have them think about what it'll be like to be much older.

Ask:

What responsibilities will you have? What freedoms?

Assign each group one tree on the handout to complete. After a few minutes, have each group report its answers.

4. *I am the vine, you are the branches*—(You'll need a plant cutting for each person.) Give each person a plant cutting. Ask kids to think about what chance these cuttings have to survive without being connected to the plant or without having roots.

Say: **We need to be connected also—to our families and to Christ. Our families have expectations of us and Christ has expectations of us.**

Ask kids to think about these ideas as you do this activity.

Tell group members you're going to read and act out a Bible passage. They're to repeat everything you say and do. Read aloud the passage on page 79 and include the appropriate motions. Pause after each phrase-and-motion combination and allow time for it to be repeated:

After the reading, have kids get in groups of three. Draw their attention to the incomplete sentences taped on the wall. Have each person select two sentences, complete them aloud, and discuss them with his or her group.

5. *Rooted in Christ, rooted in love*—(You'll need a large plastic-foam cup and a marker for each person.) Say: **To branch out healthy and strong and to bear much fruit, we must be well-rooted. Our roots begin to grow when we're born and they're nurtured by those who care for us—parents,**

From Tiny Seedling to Great Tree

Instructions: Under your assigned tree, write three freedoms and three responsibilities you had, have or expect to have at that time in your life. As other groups report, fill in the blanks under the other trees.

Toddler
freedoms

Third-grader
freedoms

Now
freedoms

responsibilities

responsibilities

responsibilities

High school senior
freedoms

College student
freedoms

Adult
freedoms

responsibilities

responsibilities

responsibilities

John 15:5-11

I am the vine, (make swaying motion)

you (point to group)

are the branches. (hold arms outstretched from shoulders)

If a man remains in me, (hug person next to you)

and I in him, (get person next to you to hug you)

he will bear much fruit; (make lifting motion)

for apart from me (cross arms, turn back on group)

you can do nothing. (cross arms, wave hands in front of you)

If anyone does not remain in me, (turn, gently push away person you hugged)

he is like a branch that is thrown away (make throwing motion)

and withers; (make withering motion)

such branches are picked up, (make gathering motion)

thrown into the fire (make throwing motion)

and burned. (jump away as if you were burned)

If you remain in me (hug person next to you)

and my words remain in you, (hug person next to you)

ask whatever you wish, (reach hand out with palm open)

and it will be given you. (close hand, bring to chest)

This is to my Father's glory, (raise hands to heaven)

that you bear much fruit, (hold arms out, lifting)

showing yourselves to be my disciples. (put your arms around the people next to you)

As the Father has loved me, (point to heaven)

so have I loved you. (place your crossed hands on your chest)

Now remain in my love, (put arms around those people near you)

If you obey my commands, (make emphasizing gesture on obey)

you will remain in my love, (put arms around those near you)

just as I have obeyed (point to self)

my Father's commands (point to heaven)

and remain in his love. (hug self)

I have told you this so that my joy may be in you (take someone's hands and dance that person around)

and that your joy may be complete. (jump around and cheer)

brothers and sisters, other family members, friends, teachers and ministers. We're rooted in the values we learn, the traditions we grow up with and the relationships we build.

Give each person a plastic-foam cup and a marker. Have kids each draw six large roots on their cup or divide their cup into six sections for writing. Have them each write the following things in the six roots or sections. Write the list on newsprint and tape it on the wall:

(1) all their family members' names;

(2) family traditions (for example, going to grandparents' for Christmas, devotions after supper or special dinner after church);

(3) values their family stands for;

(4) things their family enjoys doing;

(5) how their family helps other people; and

(6) how their family shares Christ with one another.

On the bottom of their cup, have kids each write one thing they need to do to strengthen their root system or keep it growing strong. Form groups of three again, and have kids share what they wrote. Have kids save their cups.

6. *Bearing much fruit*—(You'll need construction paper, scissors, markers and masking tape.) Have kids each think about where they are in their journey of branching out from their family. Have them each cut out a construction paper fruit that represents where they are in their quest for freedom and responsibility. For example, someone might cut out a banana to show how he or she is slowly "peeling" away from his or her family. Ask:

● **What does it mean to "bear much fruit"?**

● **What kind of fruit do you want to produce?**

On their fruit, have kids each write what they plan to do to bear much fruit.

Have everyone sit in a circle around the tree. Have each person share why he or she chose that fruit and what's written on it, and then tape the fruit on the tree.

7. *Closing*—(You'll need potting soil and seeds.) Have kids each stand in a circle and hold their cup. Put potting soil in each cup and give each person a seed. Read aloud John 15:16 as kids plant their seeds.

Pray for group members to bear fruit in Christ's name as they branch out in freedom and responsibility.

Celebrate with refreshments.

11 *Family Feelings*

By Ann Cannon

Junior highers may have several different feelings toward family members: appreciation, frustration, respect, anger.

Use this meeting to let kids share feelings about their families and hear how other kids struggle and cope with their families.

OBJECTIVES

Participants will:
- identify feelings toward family members;
- examine ways to improve feelings toward their families;

and

- affirm positive feelings about their families.

BEFORE THE MEETING

Read the meeting, collect supplies and photocopy handouts.

Photocopy "Game Statements" and cut apart the statements for activity #1.

If possible, videotape some people acting out the "Family Feud" scenes in activity #3. If you don't have the equipment, plan to have several junior highers role-play the scenes during the meeting.

Set up the video equipment.

THE MEETING

1. *Introduce family feelings*—(For each person you'll need a game statement cut apart from the "Game Statements" handout on page 82.) Start junior highers thinking about their

82

Game Statements

✂ -

● Teenagers should be allowed to decorate their own rooms.	● Junior highers should set their own curfews.
● Junior highers shouldn't be responsible for cleaning their rooms.	● You should treat a stepmother like your real mother.
● A stepfather shouldn't discipline his stepchildren.	● Single parents shouldn't expect their teenagers to clean and cook.
● Sisters who wear the same size should share clothes.	● Brothers get along best with younger sisters.
● Parents are less strict with their youngest child.	● Parents are less strict with their oldest child.
● Sisters get along better than brothers.	● Brothers compete with each other.
● Girls get along better with their dads than with their moms.	● Parents don't play favorites with their children.
● Guys get along better with their dads than with their moms.	● Junior highers who have a single parent usually don't want their parent to remarry.
● Junior highers who have a single parent usually want their parent to remarry.	● Parents spoil an only child.
● Parents should include their teenage children when deciding about a job change or moving.	● Teenagers don't worry about family problems.
● Teenagers can control their feelings.	● Teenagers can't control their feelings.
● Parents should meet a teenager's friends.	● It isn't necessary to tell a parent everywhere you go.
● Single-parent kids relate better to their parent since they deal with only one parent.	● Junior highers with divorced parents shouldn't be forced to spend time with both parents.
● A teenager doesn't need a regular allowance.	● Stepsisters who are the same age get along well.

feelings toward their families. As each person arrives, give him or her a slip of paper with a game statement on it.

After a few minutes, tell kids to sit on the floor in groups of four. Have groups each read their slips of paper and discard one statement everyone disagrees with. Then have each group of four combine with another group. Have the groups of eight read their statements and discard another everyone disagrees with. Each group of eight should end up with five cards.

Have group members talk about each remaining statement. Have kids place the statements they all agree with in a pile; the statements some members agree with and some don't in a second pile; and the statements no one agrees with in a third pile.

Call the groups together and ask:

● **Which statement did everyone agree on immediately?**

● **Which statement was the most controversial? Why?**

2. *Itemize family feelings*—(You'll need newsprint and a marker. For each person, you'll need a "Family Feelings Inventory" and a pencil.) Say: **Based on your discussions, name feelings junior highers have toward their families.**

Ask someone to list responses on newsprint. Give everyone a "Family Feelings Inventory" and a pencil. Tell kids to complete the inventory to evaluate their personal feelings toward their families. After a few minutes, ask:

● **What feelings from your inventories could we add to the newsprint list?**

● **How do you feel knowing that others often have feelings similar to yours?**

3. *Intervene in family feuds*—(You'll need the videotaped "family feud" scenes, or kids to role-play the situations. For each person, you'll need a Bible.) As you direct attention toward the videotaped scenes or role plays, ask junior highers to think about how they'd feel in each situation. Hand out Bibles. After each scene, stop and ask questions.

Scene 1: One night at dinner, Dad teases Jorey about using makeup for the first time. Jorey tries to ignore the teasing, but then her brother joins in.

Ask:

● **How would you feel if you were Jorey?**

● **How do you react to family teasing?**

84

Family Feelings Inventory

Part I

Disgust   Anger   Fear   Frustration   Ignore   Dislike   Don't care
Put up with   Like   Respect   Polite   Concern   Appreciate   Enjoy   Adore

Instructions: Everyone has different feelings toward each family member. Write five emotions you usually feel toward each family member. Under "1" write the feeling you have most often and under "5," the feeling you have least often. Use the feelings suggested above or add your own.

Name	1	2	3	4	5
_____	_____	_____	_____	_____	_____
_____	_____	_____	_____	_____	_____
_____	_____	_____	_____	_____	_____
_____	_____	_____	_____	_____	_____
_____	_____	_____	_____	_____	_____
_____	_____	_____	_____	_____	_____
_____	_____	_____	_____	_____	_____
_____	_____	_____	_____	_____	_____

continued

Part II

Instructions: Complete the statements assigned to your group.

An attitude that would help me get along better with my family is . . .

One thing I can change about the way I feel toward my family is . . .

I need to say I'm sorry when . . .

I should compliment my _____ when . . .

I can help my family trust me by . . .

I can improve my relationship with my _____ by . . .

I need my family because . . .

When I have a teenager, I'll . . .

I could demonstrate maturity to my family by . . .

I could improve family communication by . . .

Read aloud Ephesians 6:4. Ask:

● **How does Ephesians 6:4 relate to this scene?**

Scene 2: Pat and Mike are brothers. Today Mike was kicked off the basketball team for poor grades. Mike takes out his anger at himself on Pat.

Ask:

● **How would you feel if you were Pat?**

● **How do you handle a family member's disappointment?**

Read aloud Proverbs 17:17 and 18:19. Ask:

● **How do Proverbs 17:17 and 18:19 relate to this scene?**

Scene 3: Juanice comes home two hours past curfew to find her father waiting up. Juanice tries to defend her tardiness, but her dad won't listen.

Ask:

● **How would you feel if you were Juanice?**

● **How do you react when you know you've done something wrong?**

Read aloud Proverbs 13:1 and Ephesians 6:1. Ask:

● **How do Proverbs 13:1 and Ephesians 6:1 relate to this scene?**

4. *Improve family feelings*—(For each person you'll need the "Family Feelings Inventory" used in activity #2 and a pencil.) Explain that group members can improve their feelings toward their families. Ask kids to look at Part II of the "Family Feelings Inventory." Form groups of no more than six, each with an adult sponsor. Divide the statements among the groups. Ask each group to complete its statement(s) with its best advice.

When groups are ready, have them share responses with the total group. Urge everyone to write each group's advice on the inventories. Encourage kids to keep these inventories to review how to improve family feelings.

5. *Inspire family ties*—(You'll need a ball of string.) Thank group members for sharing during this meeting. Explain that it's easy to criticize, but it's better to remember the good things.

Have group members and sponsors stand in a circle. Tie the end of a ball of string around your wrist and pass the ball to the next person. Instruct group members each to wrap the string loosely around one wrist. As they're wrapping the string around a wrist, have kids each tell something positive about their family or relate an enjoyable family activity.

After the ball of string has gone around the circle, read aloud Colossians 2:2-3. Say: **We're drawn together by our love for one another and our love for Jesus. He's the secret for learning how to form positive family feelings.**

Close by singing "We Are the Family of God," *Songs* (Songs and Creations).

12 A Family-Ties Surprise

By Karen Dockrey

"You don't understand," screams Jennifer. "Susie and Tamara are expecting me at the party tonight!"

"I do understand," retorts Jennifer's mom. "I understand you haven't finished cleaning your room, and I said you couldn't go until the job was done."

"But mom, I'm half finished, and I can work after school tomorrow to finish it," pleads Jennifer.

"Finish it now, then go," her mom responds.

Jennifer storms upstairs, muttering through clenched teeth, "You . . . don't . . . understand."

Why don't parents and kids understand each other? It's usually a matter of perspective. Kids are forming relationships, having fun and learning to be independent. Parents are deepening relationships, meeting daily obligations and staying responsible.

Use this meeting to help kids and parents see things from each other's perspective. Help them work through problems from a new vantage point. And encourage them to appreciate one another.

OBJECTIVES

Participants will:

● play a blindfold game to discover blind spots that keep them from open communication and compassionate understanding;

● fill out charts to help kids and parents understand how they perceive each other;

● play a game to help kids and parents talk about things they struggle to understand about each other; and

● commit to at least one concrete action they can take to promote understanding in their homes.

BEFORE THE MEETING

Read the meeting, collect supplies and photocopy handouts.

Invite kids and their parents to the meeting at least one month in advance. If possible, have parents R.S.V.P. so you'll know exactly who'll be there.

Recruit two adult volunteers to ask questions during The Family-Ties Game.

Purchase an inexpensive handkerchief for each participant. Or ask kids and parents each to bring a handkerchief they can write on.

Set up three to five pairs of chairs in the front of the room. Make a sign that reads "The Family-Ties Game," and tape it on the wall behind the chairs.

Pray for unity between parents and kids, and invite one or more people to pray with you.

THE MEETING

1. *Finding the blinders*—(You'll need a handkerchief blindfold and a marker for each person.) As kids and parents enter, give each a blindfold and a marker. Say: **Write on your blindfold at least 10 areas of blindness, or lack of understanding, between kids and parents. These can be areas you fight over at home or ones that are common to all kids and parents.**

After 10 minutes, tell parents and kids to put on their blindfolds and make sure they can't see. Say: **When I call out a number, I want you to lock arms in a circle of that number of people. Here's the catch: You can't say anything to** find each other. For example, if I yell "five," you should silently find four other people to lock arms with in a circle.

Call out three or four different numbers, one at a time, and end by calling out the number three. When kids and parents have linked arms in trios, tell participants to remove their blindfolds, sit down in their groups and discuss the areas of blindness they wrote on their blindfolds.

After a discussion time, ask:

How is a blindfold like a misunderstanding between parents and kids?

Say: **Often when we disagree, we feel like the other person can't or won't open his or her eyes. And sometimes when we take off our blindfolds, we squint at the light. For example, we don't like what we now understand, and so we react negatively. We respond by saying something that will keep the blindfolds up between us. But we can take the blindfold off and use it for positive purposes such as cleaning a hurt or bandaging a wound. Put away your blindfolds for now; we'll use them again later.**

2. *The perception connection*—(You'll need a "Junior Higher Perceptions" handout for each young person, an "Adult Perceptions" handout for each parent and a pencil for each person.) Give kids and adults pencils and the appropriate handouts, and ask them each to complete each exercise and answer the questions.

After kids and parents finish their handouts, ask a few volunteers to tell about their perceptions. Then ask:

● **How are our perceptions of each other different today from when kids were 3 years old? 5 years old? 10 years old?**

● **How do kids' and parents' perceptions of each other today differ?** (For example, parents might consider their junior higher a child, but kids may see themselves as more grown up.)

● **How do our perceptions of each other affect the way we understand or fail to understand each other?**

● **How can we find out whether our perceptions are accurate?**

Say: **The more we share our perceptions, fears, hopes and ideas, the better we understand each other and the**

Junior Higher Perceptions

Instructions: Doodle, draw or write the way you saw your parents when you were these ages. Include feelings, shared events, words, fun times, hard experiences or whatever memories come to mind.

Age 3:	Age 5:
Age 10:	Today:

How do your memories of your parents affect how you feel about them today?

How do your parents' memories of you affect how they feel about you today?

92

Adult Perceptions

Instructions: Doodle, draw or write the way you saw your junior higher when he or she was these ages. Include feelings, shared events, words, fun times, hard experiences or whatever memories come to mind.

Age 3:	Age 5:
Age 10:	**Today:**

How do your memories of your junior higher affect how you feel about him or her today?

How do your junior higher's memories of you affect the way he or she feels about you today?

better we communicate. Let's have some fun learning to communicate.

3. *The Family-Ties Game*—(You'll need nine 8½ × 11 pieces of construction paper or posterboard and a marker for each person in the game. You'll also need newsprint and two more markers. For the winning pair you'll need a "Family-Ties" blue ribbon you design, or a meal from a fast-food restaurant.) Ask for three to five parent-young person pairs to volunteer for the game. Don't pick more than five pairs.

Say: **You've heard of** *The Dating Game* **and** *The Newlywed Game.* **But today we're going one step further. It's time for The Family-Ties Game! We'll find out how much kids and their parents really know about each other. What bugs them? What do they really like about each other? What's behind their struggles and joys? Let's have our parent-young person pairs come on up and sit in the game chairs. Each of you should pick up nine posterboard cards and a marker from me.**

Say to the people participating in the game: **In a moment, you'll leave the room with an adult leader and privately answer the same questions we'll ask your partner. Then we'll have you come back here to see just how well you know each other.**

Assign a questioner to each group. At this point, you have three groups with three leaders: Parents, Kids and Audience. Give leaders each a copy of the "Family-Ties Game" handout. Send the kids participating in the game to one room and the parents to another room. Have the leaders follow the instructions on the handout.

Call time when the adult questioners tell you that the game participants have finished their private answers. Announce that both teams have excellent lists, lightly mention the winner, and ask the teams to roll up their lists and let no one see them until you ask for them.

Have the adult questioners bring in the kids and parents. Parents and kids should sit together in pairs. Encourage applause. Have the questioner assigned to the parents ask the kids the questions asked the parents privately. The questioner should encourage the kids to answer the way they think their parents answered. After each young person answers, cue the matching parent to lift the card that answers the question. Award 20 points for answers that match. For the last two questions, award 40

94

Family-Ties Game

Instructions: Cut apart each set of instructions and give to the appropriate leader.

● **Parents' Leader:** Ask the following questions and instruct parents to write their answers on their posterboard cards. Parents should keep their answers hidden from the others. Note: You may use all or just some of the questions listed. The questions alternate between affirmation and problem areas.
   1. I worry most about . . .
   2. I show my junior higher I love him or her by . . .
   3. I get most frustrated with my junior higher when . . .
   4. I'm really proud of my junior higher because . . .
   5. I think my junior higher doesn't understand me when . . .
   6. My junior higher is happiest when . . .
   7. I know I fail my junior higher when . . .
   8. I trust my junior higher when . . .
   9. I most want my junior higher to know that I . . .

✂ -

● **Kids' Leader:** Ask the following questions and instruct the kids to write their answers on their cards. Kids should keep their answers hidden from the others. Note: You may use all or just some of the questions listed. The questions alternate between affirmation and problem areas.
   1. I worry most about . . .
   2. I show my parent I love him or her by . . .
   3. I get most frustrated with my parent when . . .
   4. I'm really proud of my parent because . . .
   5. I think my parent doesn't understand when . . .
   6. My parent is happiest when . . .
   7. I know I fail my parent when . . .
   8. I trust my parent when . . .
   9. I most want my parent to know that I . . .

- -

● **Audience's Leader:** Divide the audience into two teams (mix parents and kids evenly). Give each team newsprint and a marker. Say: **Each team should try to make a list of ''communication clearers'' that's longer than the other team's. Communication clearers are ways to take off our blindfolds, to understand each other, to encourage each other. Think of things that would help you live together better at home.**

points for matching answers. Encourage unity by pointing out how close the answers were.

Repeat the process with the questioner assigned to the kids asking parents the kids' questions.

Encourage sensitivity and fun. Point out that we really are alike in our struggles to understand each other at home. Emphasize that sometimes kids have as much trouble understanding parents as parents do understanding them. Award the winning pair a free fast-food meal or a "Family-Ties" blue ribbon.

After the game is over and a winner is determined, say: **Parents and kids don't always understand each other precisely. To help out, our audience has come up with some ideas to improve communication and strengthen ties.**

Have audience team members call out some ideas from their lists that they think would help the game participants.

4. *Healing the blindness*—Form a circle. Have participants each take out their handkerchief and circle three areas of blindness they want to remove in their family. Have kids and parents each say aloud an area of blindness and the action they plan to take to remove it. After each person talks, have everyone say "amen." Tell kids and parents to keep their handkerchiefs in a prominent place as a reminder of their commitment.

13 Why Do My Parents Embarrass Me?

By Ann Cannon

According to Dr. G. Keith Olson, family therapist, when parents unintentionally "embarrass" their junior higher, the junior higher reveals how he or she still feels tied to them. Dr. Olson says kids assume that "the onlookers, particularly friends, will decide that 'if the parents say stupid things, the kid must be stupid too'; 'if the parents aren't as respected as my parents, the kid must not be good enough to be my friend'; 'if the parents do strange things, the kids must be weird too.' "

Junior highers struggle for identity; they don't take risks with the image they want to present. So when parents seemingly ruin the image, kids respond with embarrassment—as if they themselves had blundered.

Over time, you can help junior highers understand how you outgrew feeling embarrassed about your parents—how as kids' identity and independence grow, they no longer feel embarrassed about their parents.

Use this meeting to examine embarrassing situations and ways to deal with them.

OBJECTIVES

Participants will:
- determine feelings toward parents in specific situations;
- discover why they feel embarrassed;
- suggest ways to deal with embarrassment; and
- hear ways to reduce embarrassment.

BEFORE THE MEETING

Read the meeting, collect supplies and photocopy handouts.

For activity #1, gather slides of the parents of kids who normally attend. Ask for slides of parents in silly situations. Look through camp, retreat or party slides for those of parents who chaperoned. Or take some slides of parents in funny clothing, unusual situations, doing stunts or making crazy faces.

For each guy you'll need a slip of paper labeled either "F" or "S"; for each girl, a slip of paper labeled either "M" or "D." These will be used in activity #2.

For activity #6, write on four separate posters one of these headings: "Dear Blabby," "The Phil Donahue Show," "Family Mailbox" and "Sound Advice." Attach an envelope to each poster. Create equal numbers of four different-color "tickets" (pieces of paper), each with a title from the posters written on it—enough for each group member to have one. Place each in the envelope that corresponds to its label.

THE MEETING

1. Slides—(You'll need the slides of parents and a projector.) Show the slides. Listen to kids' remarks as you show the slides. Ask how the kids feel seeing their parents. When you finish showing the slides, repeat several remarks you heard during the slides. Ask:

Why are kids sometimes embarrassed by their parents?

2. Embarrassing situations—(For each guy, you'll need a slip of paper labeled either "F" or "S"; for each girl, you'll need slips labeled either "M" or "D.") Hand out labeled slips of paper to the group. Explain that those with "F" or "M" are fathers or mothers; those with "S" or "D" are sons or daughters. Have kids form "family groups" with one to three children, based on the slips. Some kids can form single-parent family groups.

Tell family groups each to think of a situation in which their parents embarrass them. For example: eating out with parents; parents' actions at a school event; or shopping with parents. After a few minutes, call on each family group to act out its situation.

Explain that in this meeting you'll talk about ways to handle being embarrassed by parents.

3. *Identifying feelings*—(You'll need five signs taped to different areas of the ceiling, each with one of these statements written on it: "Totally Embarrassed," "Slightly Embarrassed," "Frustrated," "Hurt" and "No Problem!") Point out the signs taped to the ceiling. Tell kids for each situation you read, they should stand under the sign that best expresses their feelings. For each situation, ask why kids chose as they did. Read the situations:

● **Your mom is pregnant.**

● **Your mom criticizes your clothes in front of your best friend.**

● **Your dad tries to talk your language, but gets it all wrong.**

● **You receive a special award at school and your parents come, even though you didn't invite them (the principal did).**

● **Your dad calls your math teacher to discuss an argument you had with the teacher.**

4. *Discussing feelings*—(For each person you'll need a "Who Me, Embarrassed?" handout and a pencil. For each group, you'll need a Bible.) Have kids sit with their family groups again. Hand out "Who Me, Embarrassed?" Give each family group a Bible. Direct the person with the shortest hair in each family group to lead the discussion of the questions in Part A.

5. *Embarrassed Bible people*—Ask the oldest person in each family group to lead Part B of the handout.

Ask a representative from each family group to report ideas.

6. *Solutions*—(Tape the labeled posters and envelopes with tickets in them on separate walls. You'll also need these supplies set out on a table: paper, pencils, markers, construction paper and a shoe box. Also set on the table a copy of each of the four "Solution Projects.") To discover ways to deal with embarrassing

99

Who Me, Embarrassed?

Instructions: Discuss these questions and statements in your family group.

Part A

Discuss:
- Which situation you've seen or heard about today would most embarrass you? Why?
- Are others embarrassed by your parents' actions? Explain.
- Why are you more embarrassed by your parents when you're around your friends than when you're alone?
- How does your embarrassment make you feel about your relationship with your parents?

Part B

1. Have someone read aloud John 9:1, 6-7, 18-23 as the others listen for how the parents felt. Discuss:
- Why were the parents embarrassed about their son's healing?
- How is this a case of reverse embarrassment (parents embarrassed by their child)?
- When are your parents embarrassed by you?

2. Have someone read aloud Luke 2:41-49 as the others listen for the parents' feelings and Jesus' feelings. Discuss:
- Was Jesus embarrassed? Why or why not?
- How does Jesus' reaction to his parents compare with yours?

situations with parents, let kids choose a project from the posters with these titles: "Dear Blabby," "The Phil Donahue Show," "Family Mailbox" and "Sound Advice." Have each kid choose a ticket. Kids will need to make a second selection if tickets for their first choice are gone.

Direct ticket-holders to form four teams under one of the labeled posters. Give each team a copy of its solution project. Point out the supply table. Tell teams they have 10 minutes to complete their project.

After 10 minutes, let each team share its project with the whole group.

7. *A step further*—(You'll need a sheet of newsprint with

100

Solution Projects

● **Dear Blabby**—Write a response to the following letter as if you were a famous advice columnist.

Dear Blabby,

My parents drive me crazy! They try to embarrass me. The other night at a nice restaurant, my dad kidded the waiter about how expensive everything was. At first, the waiter thought he was serious; it was so embarrassing! It's also embarrassing when everyone else's parents come to the game to see them play, but my parents are too busy. What can I do when my parents embarrass me? I love them, but . . .

Confused

Choose someone to read your letter to the whole group.

● **The Phil Donahue Show**—Prepare a debate between Phil and a guest who believes "the average teenager shouldn't be embarrassed by parents."

Your team must play both the roles of Phil and his guest. So prepare questions for Phil to ask and responses for the guest to make. Also prepare a few questions for the guest to ask Phil.

For example, the guest might say: "A teenager spends most of his time away from his parents, so how can he or she be embarrassed?" or "Peers influence teenagers more than parents."

Phil might ask: "But when teenagers have to go out with their parents, why do parents embarrass them with their actions?" or "Which is more important—a kid's relationship with parents or friends? Why?"

Be prepared to present your debate.

● **Family Mailbox**—Design a logo for a family mailbox (use the shoe box) that suggests how to feel comfortable with parents. Choose a catchy slogan about living through embarrassment. Or develop a symbol that gives advice to teenagers embarrassed by parents.

Be prepared to explain your creation to the whole group.

● **Sound Advice**—Using the tune of a commercial jingle or a popular song, write a song that offers advice on how to deal with parents who are embarrassing.

Be prepared to sing your sound advice to the whole group.

these phrases written on it: Work at being independent; Control your feelings; Have a good self-image; and Use positive remarks to show you appreciate parents.) Gather everyone in a circle. Display the sheet of newsprint with the phrases written on it. Discuss each point. Include these ideas:

● One task of growing up is to develop independence from your family. That isn't easy. It sometimes makes you uncomfortable with your family, because you're forming your own ideas, thoughts and values.

● You tend to become angry, hostile or too excited. As you grow, you learn more about how to control your reactions.

● When you like yourself, you're more accepting of others. When you don't like yourself, you see others' faults more quickly.

● Your situation will likely improve when you give parents sincere compliments instead of criticism.

Ask:

What are positive comments you could say to your parents? (For example, "Thanks for being here when I need you" or "I love you because you're you.")

Challenge kids each to choose one statement on the poster to work on during the week. Have kids find partners and share their chosen statements. Have partners suggest things to do about the statements.

8. *A final look*—Gather everyone in a circle. Have group members each say one positive thing about their parents or one thing they're thankful for about their parents. Close by thanking God for parents of these terrific young people.

Section Four:

FAITH

14 Does God Really Love Me?

By Paula Mott-Becker

G od's most powerful message of his love is in the person of Jesus Christ. Christ's unconditional love is of primary importance to junior highers who feel unaccepted.

Use this meeting to help junior highers understand that God loves them without expecting anything in return.

OBJECTIVES

Participants will:
● play a game showing how people place conditions on giving love;
● discover the qualities of unconditional love;
● see Christ as God's expression of unconditional love; and
● tell how various items remind them that God cares for them.

BEFORE THE MEETING

Read the meeting, collect supplies and photocopy handouts.

For activity #2, photocopy and cut apart the "Love Cards" and "Kindness Cards." You'll need a stack of 30 "love" cards and a set of 12 different "kindness" cards for every two group members. You'll also need some upbeat "love" background music to play during the activity.

For activity #4, obtain the film, *Greater Love* (from Mass Me-

104

"Love" Cards Pattern

Love	Love	Love	Love	Love
Love	Love	Love	Love	Love
Love	Love	Love	Love	Love

dia Ministries, 2116 N. Charles St., Baltimore, MD 21218, 301-727-3270). You'll also need a film projector and screen.

For activity #7, fill a box with assorted items such as a leaf, mirror, fruit, a quarter, paper cup, balloon, string, pencil, a flower, bubble gum (make sure you have more items than kids who'll be at the meeting; it's okay to have duplicates).

THE MEETING

1. *Arrival*—Be available to meet junior highers as they arrive. Spend time talking casually with them about their week at school or home.

2. *Love for trade*—(You'll need stacks of "love" and "kindness" cards and upbeat "love" background music.) Say: **This game will help group members look at how we place values on things people do for us.**

Divide the group in half by having kids number off "love, kindness, love, kindness," and so on. Give each "love" a stack of

"Kindness" Cards Pattern

Buys lunch for you	Listens to your problems	Shares class notes with you	Loans you money
Helps with homework	Lets you borrow clothes	Buys you candy	Goes shopping with you
Says nice things about you	Invites you to a party	Forgives you when you've caused hurt	Goes to the movies with you

Permission to photocopy these cards granted for local church use. Copyright © 1989 by Thom Schultz Publications, Inc., Box 481, Loveland, CO 80539.

30 "love" cards. Give the "kindnesses" each a stack of 12 different "kindness" cards. Give all instructions to both groups. Once the trading begins, kids may assume either role because they'll have both kinds of cards.

Instructions for "kindness" card group:

● **Begin the trading by offering your kindness cards in trade for love cards.**

● **When you're offered a certain number of love cards for a kindness card, you may accept them or try to get more love cards for your kindness card.**

● **You may trade with anyone as often as you like.**

Instructions for the "love" card group:

● **You must read the kindness card being offered and determine its value. You must decide how many love cards that kindness is worth.**

● **You may trade for as many kindnesses as you want.**

● **You may turn down an opportunity to trade.**

● **You may trade for the same kindness as many times as you want.**

Instructions for both groups:

● **As soon as the trading begins you'll have both kinds of cards. You may offer kindness or give love by trading either kind of card.**

During the trading, play upbeat "love" music. Let kids move around freely. Allow 10 to 15 minutes for trading.

Call time and get the group members together in a circle. Ask:

● **Which did you like better, giving love or offering kindness? Was one easier to do than the other? Why or why not?**

● **How did you feel when you didn't get as many love cards as you wanted for a kindness?**

● **Which kindnesses seemed to be valued the most? Why?**

● **How is this game like real life?**

● **What are some times when others have placed conditions on their love for you?** (For example, "I'll invite you to my party if you'll help me with my homework.")

● **Is it possible to love someone without conditions? Why or why not?**

3. *A question of love*—(For each person, you'll need a 3×5 card and a pencil.) Say: **Unconditional love isn't easy to find in our world. Sometimes our pets are the best examples of "no strings attached" love. Parents can also be examples. If you wanted to find out if a person really loved you unconditionally, what questions would you ask that person?**

Hand out pencils and 3×5 cards. Have kids each write at least two questions on their 3×5 card. Collect the questions and read them to the whole group. Have group members think of people in their lives who could answer each question positively. Share an experience from your life when someone loved you unconditionally and what that meant to you. Encourage the junior highers to share also.

4. *Greater love*—(You'll need the *Greater Love* film and a projector. For each person, you'll need a "*Greater Love* Discussion Questions" handout and a pencil.) Unconditional love gives everything and expects nothing in return. The film *Greater Love* gives an example of unconditional love. In the film a little girl gives blood to help her sick brother. She gives the blood believ-

Greater Love *Discussion Questions*

1. What feelings do you think the little girl had before she realized she wouldn't die?

2. How do you think the brother felt when he found out his sister was willing to give her life for him?

3. What effect do you think this event had on the other family members?

4. How would you describe the love the little girl had for her brother?

5. Why is that kind of love such a surprise? Why is it so highly valued?

Permission to photocopy this handout granted for local church use. Copyright © 1989 by Thom Schultz Publications, Inc., Box 481, Loveland, CO 80539.

ing that it will make her die.

Show the film. Then form groups of four to six with an adult sponsor in each group. Give each group a *"Greater Love Discussion Questions"* handout. Have kids discuss the film.

5. *The greatest love*—Say: **When everyone and everything else in life fails us, Jesus will be there for us. He's the truest and best example of unconditional love.**

Have everyone form a circle. Have someone read aloud John 15:12-17. Say: **Jesus calls us his friends. He wants a relationship of love and trust with each of us. To show his love, he gave up his life and died on the cross. We don't deserve his love; we can't earn his love; but we can accept it by loving him back and loving other people. God's message of love goes something like this: "I'll always love you. Don't be afraid that I'll ever take my love from you. Nothing you can think, feel, say or do will change my love for you. I won't reject you. I won't go back on my promise. My love for you doesn't depend on what you've done or promise to do. I give my love as a gift. I want your love in return, but my love remains even if you don't accept it."**

6. *Love is*—(For each person, you'll need three sheets of red construction paper, scissors and a marker.) Hand out three sheets of red construction paper, scissors and a marker to each group member. Have each group member make three hearts and

108

write "Love is . . ." on them. Tape the hearts on the wall and let group members each finish three sentences by writing their own definitions on the hearts. Allow time for kids to read the completed sentences.

Read aloud 1 Corinthians 13. Discuss any ideas that were missed in the sentences on the hearts. Add any that should've been included.

7. *The gift*—(You'll need the box of assorted items.) God shows his love in many ways. All creation is a symbol of God's love for us. Bring in the box of assorted items. Have the group members sit in a circle around the box. Have group members each choose an item and tell how the item reminds them of God's love for them. For example, a paper cup could remind them of how God always fills their lives with love.

Encourage group members each to keep their item and share its meaning with their family and friends.

15 Getting to Know God

By Rick Lawrence

If you give kids information about God, some will remember it, some won't. But if you help kids experience God in your meeting room, few will leave unchanged. Despite their typical outward signs of rebellion, junior highers hunger for answers to the deep things that trouble them.

That's because the junior high years are a shotgun blast of change, challenge and choices. "Because my parents do it that way" isn't the rock-solid reason it used to be. Junior highers cautiously pull up anchor and move away from their parental pier, just to see if the boat will float. Somewhere along the way, they'll decide whether to draw closer to God or reject him.

Richard Foster wrote a classic book on spiritual growth called *Celebration of Discipline*. In it, he outlines 12 practical disciplines that lead to intimacy with God. Use this meeting, based on some of Foster's disciplines, to help kids understand and know God.

110

OBJECTIVES

Participants will:

● learn how distractions and busyness can block out God's voice;

● experience five ways they can know and understand God;

● evaluate their lifestyle to see who or what's in control of them; and

● learn how to listen to God in quiet.

BEFORE THE MEETING

Read the meeting, collect supplies and photocopy handouts.

In activity #2 you'll need a small flower or flower sticker for each person.

THE MEETING

1. *What'd you say?*—(You'll need some "treasure" to hide such as a plate of cookies or granola bars. You'll also need a name tag that reads "Mouth," a name tag that reads "Ear," news-print, a marker, and for each person a 3×5 card and a pencil.) Hide the treasure in a place where your group can make plenty of noise. Have two volunteers play a communication game. Put the Mouth name tag on one and the Ear name tag on the other. Have the volunteers stand at opposite ends of the room or meeting area. Have the remaining group members form a circle around the person with the Mouth name tag.

Say: **Somewhere in this meeting area is a treasure. The goal of Mouth is to give Ear directions to the treasure so they can both enjoy it. The goal of everyone else is to keep Ear from accurately hearing Mouth's directions so the remaining group members can split the treasure among themselves. After I whisper the directions to the treasure in Mouth's ear, he or she will have two minutes to communicate the directions to Ear. Everyone else should make the loudest racket possible to drown out Mouth's directions. If Ear can't find the treasure in two minutes, everyone else wins. Mouth can't leave the circle, and Ear can't get within 15 feet of the circle.**

Give Mouth some moderately difficult directions to the hidden treasure. Tell kids when they can start, and stop the game after two minutes. Make sure Ear never gets closer than 15 feet from the circle. After the game is over, gather everyone together.

Have the kids who played the parts of Ear and Mouth talk about their biggest frustrations with the game. Ask the kids who formed the circle to brainstorm ideas that would've helped Ear listen better to the directions—such as less noise or shorter distance between Ear and Mouth. List their ideas on newsprint. Ask:

How was our treasure hunt like God trying to talk to us?

Say: **We live in a society that's full of noises and distractions. Sometimes we're so busy with activities or commitments that it's hard to hear what God is trying to say to us, even when he's shouting. The best way to hear what God has to say is to remove some of the noise and distraction from our lives and get closer to him. For example, if you really want to hear what God is saying, you might try cutting out one half-hour TV program a week and spend that time reading your Bible or praying. Or try fasting one meal on a certain day. Spend the mealtime reading a devotional guide, talking to a friend about God or serving someone who needs God's love.**

Distribute a 3×5 card and pencil to each person, and ask kids to list three noises or distractions that could be blocking them from hearing what God is saying.

2. *Flower power*—(You'll need two similar flowers, several "Flower Power" handouts and several copies of the poem "Miracle." For each person you'll need a small flower or flower sticker, and for each team you'll need paper and a pencil.) Form four teams of one or more people. Give each person on team #1 a "Flower Power" handout, give team #2 and team #3 each a flower, and give each person on team #4 a copy of "Miracle."

Say: **The goal of this game is to describe what makes a flower beautiful using only the information your team's been given. Each team will study a flower from a different perspective, then write a short paragraph describing its beauty.**

● **Team #1 should memorize the "Flower Power" description.**

● **Team #2 should place its flower in the middle of the group and examine it from top to bottom. You may not touch the flower or get closer than 6 inches to it.**

● **Team #3 should examine its flower closely: smell it, pull apart its petals and study its parts.**

● **Team #4 should read the poem "Miracle."**
You'll have five minutes to study and then write a
description of the flower's beauty. Then you'll read aloud
your descriptions.

Flower Power

A flower is beautiful not just for its bright color
or pleasing smell; it's beautiful for how it
makes me feel inside. A flower has the power
to bring me happiness.

Miracle

We muse on miracles who look
But lightly on a rose!
Who gives it fragrance or the glint
Of glory that it shows?

Who holds it here between the sky
And earth's rain-softened sod?
The miracle of one pale rose
Is proof enough of God!

Edith Daley

After the flower descriptions have been read, give each person a flower or a flower sticker. Ask:

How was your team's activity like getting to know
God?

Say: **Just as there are many ways to understand and de-**
scribe a flower, there are many ways we can come to un-
derstand and know God.

Ask:

● **How is examining a flower like getting to know**
God?

● **How can we understand God better?**
● **What must we do to keep our relationship with God strong?**

3. *Who's in control?*—(For each person you'll need at least one magazine, newsprint, glue, scissors, a marker and a Bible.) Pass out magazines, newsprint, glue, scissors and markers. Ask kids to cut or tear out everything they'd like to have, look like or be. After a few minutes, have kids each draw a line down the middle of their newsprint and write "I can't do without this" on one side and "I could do without this" on the other. Have kids divide the things they've chosen into the two categories without gluing them to the newsprint yet. Then gather together and have kids read aloud Matthew 6:25; Luke 12:29-34; and 1 John 5:11-12.

Say: **In light of these scriptures, look at the things you've chosen and decide whether you want to put any of them in a different category. Once you've decided, glue the pictures under the proper heading.**

Now have kids each list on their newsprint all the things they own under one or the other heading. Then gather together and read aloud Luke 16:13. Ask:

Who or what is really in control of your life?

Say: **Look over your list of personal possessions and pick one thing or one service you could give away to someone who needs it. Circle that thing on your news-print and decide who you could give it to.**

4. *Candlelit quiet*—(You'll need one large candle, matches, a flashlight, a Bible, and for each person a 3×5 card.) Distribute a 3×5 card to each person. Form a circle and place a lighted candle in the middle. Turn off the lights and use your flashlight to read aloud 1 Peter 2:13-20.

Turn off the flashlight and say: **For the next three minutes we're going to be absolutely quiet while we think of the answers to two questions. First, ask yourself if you've dis-obeyed or shown a lack of respect for someone in authority over you. Then ask God what you should do to make the situation right. When three minutes are up and I turn on the lights, write the answers to both questions on your 3×5 card.**

Ask if someone would like to talk about what he or she has written. Tell kids to take their cards home as a reminder.

5. ***Let's make a deal***—(You'll need a hat or bowl, four paper bags and one copy each of the "Famous Person's Solution" card, "I'll Trust Myself Solution" card, "Wisdom of the World Solution" card and "God's Solution" card. For each person you'll need a 3×5 card and a pencil.) Put one of the four solution cards in each of the four paper bags. Write the title of each card on the outside of the bag. Give a 3×5 card and pencil to each person. Ask kids each to write on their 3×5 card one thing they struggle with or worry about.

Collect the cards and put them in a hat or bowl. Pick one card, read the worry or concern, and ask kids which solution bag they'd pick to answer the concern. The vote must be unanimous, so kids will have to debate until they all pick the same bag. After they pick, open the bag and read the solution. Tell kids they can keep that solution or trade for what's in one of the other bags. If they trade, read the new solution. If they keep what they've got, read the other solutions to show them what they didn't trade for.

Now randomly hand out the rest of the 3×5 cards and ask each person to say a short prayer for the concern on his or her card.

Solution Cards

Instructions: Cut apart these cards.

Famous Person's Solution

Movie star Shirley MacClaine says most problems are rooted in some past life you've lived. So, if you can figure out who you were before you were you, you might find the key to your present struggle. If that doesn't work, try make-believing your problem never existed, and it will probably go away.

I'll Trust Myself Solution

Whenever you have a problem or concern, try one of the following self-help remedies: (1) Watch more television. (2) Eat more food. (3) Avoid the problem altogether. (4) Punish yourself until you feel like you've paid enough. (5) Give up. (6) Force circumstances to be the way you want them.

Wisdom of the World Solution

The world says the solution to most problems is simply to try harder. If you think you've tried as hard as you can, well, maybe you have. According to the world, some people have it and some people don't. If you're one of the have-nots, get used to it. If you're one of the haves, congratulations, you've got it made!

God's Solution

"But seek first his kingdom and his righteousness, and all these things will be given to you as well" (Matthew 6:33).

"Do not let your hearts be troubled. Trust in God; trust also in me. In my Father's house are many rooms; if it were not so, I would have told you. I am going there to prepare a place for you. And if I go and prepare a place for you, I will come back and take you to be with me that you also may be where I am. You know the way to the place where I am going . . . I am the way, and the truth and the life. No one comes to the Father except through me" (John 14:1-6).

16 *Hunting for God's Will*

By Rick Lawrence

In Charles Sheldon's Christian classic, *In His Steps,* an ordinary pastor shocks his city when he challenges his congregation to make a commitment: "I want volunteers . . . who will pledge themselves, earnestly and honestly for an entire year, not to do anything without first asking the question, 'What would Jesus do?' "

At first, only a handful of people responded to the pastor's challenge, but the explosive results of their decisions reverberated through the town. A sleepy, complacent city was suddenly roused. The scene was reminiscent of the angry mob that threatened the disciples in Acts 17: "These men who have caused trouble all over the world have now come here."

The truth is this: Your junior highers are the next generation of Christians ready to "cause trouble all over the world." But it won't happen unless they're seeking and acting upon God's will.

Use this meeting to start kids thinking about God's will and how it applies to their everyday lives.

OBJECTIVES

Participants will:

- learn what the Bible says about God's will;
- learn how to seek God's will on their own;
- pray together for God's direction in their lives; and
- do activities that will help them experience God's will.

BEFORE THE MEETING

Read the meeting and collect supplies. Create the Will Hunt Game board by photocopying pages 120 and 121. Then cut off the left edge of page 121, and overlap and tape it to the right edge of the game board on page 120. Make a copy of the game board and the "Prayer and Action Cards" for every five people. Ask kids to bring empty soft drink bottles (glass or plastic), old T-shirts and rags to the meeting. Find and bring balloons and foam-rubber scraps for pillow-making.

THE MEETING

1. *The Will Hunt Game*—(For every five people you'll need a copy of the "Will Hunt Game," a die, a Bible and a set of "Prayer and Action Cards." You'll also need a stapler and a supply of old T-shirts, foam rubber or rags, markers, tape, scissors, paper, construction paper, balloons and empty soft drink bottles.) Form groups of five, each with a mixture of guys and girls. Place all the supplies in a central location. In the middle of each group, place a copy of the "Will Hunt Game" along with the Prayer Cards and Action Cards. Have kids each find a small object (such as a piece of chalk or a pencil eraser) in the room to use as a game piece.

Say: **Though we sometimes wonder if it's possible to really know what God wants us to do in all situations, he has given us many ways to understand his will. But we won't find answers to the questions inside us unless we look for them. That's what the Will Hunt Game is all about—looking for God's answers to situations we face all the time.**

The game is simple. Each person places his or her game piece at either the GUYS or GIRLS starting line. You'll take turns rolling the die and moving the appropriate number of spaces forward. When you land on a space,

read the question aloud, find and read the Bible passage listed, then do the suggested activity as a group. If the instructions say to take an Action Card or a Prayer Card, take one, read the instructions and do the activity as a group.

You must do the suggested activity before the next person rolls the die for his or her turn. If you land on a square or take a card that your group has already answered, roll the die again and move forward. The game is over when all players have reached the finish line.

2. *Closing celebration*—(You'll need to collect all the "rescue message" bottles, youth room pillows, paper airplanes and message-filled balloons.) Have kids break the balloons, take the "rescue messages" out of the bottles, grab the youth room pillows and unfold the paper airplanes. Make sure each person has at least one item.

Have those who have a "rescue message" read the message and pray for God's help. Have those who have paper airplanes, balloon messages or pillows read their items and thank God for his love and guidance, a truth that was learned, or a good characteristic of someone in the group.

Prayer and Action Cards

✂ -

Prayer Card
Ask everyone to think about the scripture that was read; then have each person pick one thing out of that scripture that he or she is thankful for. Bow your heads and ask each person to say, "Jesus, I'm thankful for . . ."

Action Card
Have each person cut three hearts out of construction paper and write "God is alive!" on each one. Then have each person tape his or her three hearts to three people in the room.

Prayer Card
Have each person write on paper one word that expresses how he or she feels about this issue. For example, you could write "confused," "happy" or "angry." Then go around your group and have each person say, "God, I feel _____ about this."

Action Card
As a group, stand up, lock arms in a circle and shout, "God doesn't make mistakes in my life!"

Prayer Card
Draw a picture of a person, place or thing this scripture makes you think of.

Action Card
Have each person think of one characteristic that describes Jesus and complete "Jesus is . . ." on paper. Then fold the papers into airplanes and sail them toward another group.

Prayer Card
Bow your heads. Have one person say, "God, what do you think about this issue?" Then wait for one minute in silence. After one minute, have each person write on paper the first thing that occurred to him or her—no matter what it is.

Action Card
Have each person write on an old T-shirt one thing he or she appreciates about someone else in the room, and one thing he or she appreciates about God. Then staple the arms and neck of the T-shirt and stuff it full of old rags or foam rubber. Finally, staple the waist. Now you have a youth room pillow!

Prayer Card
Write God a "rescue message." Think about the issue and the scripture you just read. Now picture yourself on a desert island, needing God to rescue you from doubts, fears or confusion about this issue. Write God a rescue message such as: "God, I don't understand why my parents are getting a divorce. Help!" Then put each rescue message in a bottle and seal it. Decorate the bottle.

Action Card
Write on a slip of paper one thing you learned from the scripture passage you read. Put the paper inside a balloon, blow it up, tie it off, and thump the balloon toward another group.

PRAYER CARDS

3 Is it God's will for me to be married?
—*Read 1 Corinthians 7:7-9, 28, 32-35; then pick a Prayer Card and do as it says.*

2 Is it God's will for me to wear makeup?
—*Read 1 Peter 3:3-4; then take a Prayer Card and do what it says as a group.*

1 Is it God's will for me to be popular?
—*Read Matthew 20:20-28. Then as a group, write the answer to the question on paper.*

11 Was it God's will that a friend of mine died?
—*Read Hebrews 2:14-15; then take an Action Card and do what it says as a group.*

12 Is it God's will that I work for my allowance?
—*Read 2 Thessalonians 3:7-12. Then as a group, write the answer to the question on paper.*

13 Is it God's will that my friends have more things than me?
—*Read Hebrews 13:5-6. Then as a group, write the answer to the question on paper.*

4 Is it God's will that I have a successful career?
—*Read Romans 12:4-8; then take an Action Card and do what it says as a group.*

14

15 Is it God's will to always answer my prayers?
—*Read James 1:5-8; then take a Prayer Card and do what it says as a group.*

16 Is it God's will that I listen to rock music?
—*Read Colossians 3:16-17. Then as a group, write the answer to the question on paper.*

5 Is it God's will that I listen to rock music?
—*Read Colossians 3:16-17. Then as a group, write the answer to the question on paper.*

10 Is it God's will that people divorce?
—*Read 1 Corinthians 7:10-17; then take a Prayer Card and do what it says as a group.*

6 Is it God's will that I be happy?
—*Read James 1:2-5; then take an Action Card and do what it says as a group.*

9 Is it God's will for me to think about sex?
—*Take a Prayer Card and do what it says as a group.*

8 Is it God's will for my team to win?
—*Read Acts 10:34. Then as a group, write the answer to the question on paper.*

7 Draw an Action Card and do what it says as a group.

7 Is it God's will for me to watch R-rated movies?
—*Read Philippians 4:8. Then as a group, write the answer to the question on paper.*

6

5 Is it God's will that people starve?
—*Read Matthew 6:25-34. Then as a group, write the answer to the question on paper.*

4 Is it God's will for me to be married?
—*Read 1 Corinthians 7:7-9, 28, 32-35; then take a Prayer Card and do as it says.*

Will Hunt Game

8 Is it God's will that my body is changing and growing so fast?
—*Read 2 Samuel 23:3-5; then take a Prayer Card and do what it says as a group.*

9 Is it God's will to always answer my prayers?
—*Read James 1:5-8; then take a Prayer Card and do what it says as a group.*

10 Is it God's will for me to get good grades?
—*Read 1 Samuel 16:7; then ask your group: How are grades similar to "the outward appearance"? How well does God expect you to do in school?*

3

GUYS

1 Is it God's will that people get sick?
—*Read Philippians 2:25-30. Then as a group, write the answer to the question on paper.*

2 Is it God's will for me to fight back when others put me down?
—*Read Matthew 5:38-48; then pick a Prayer Card and pray the prayer as a group.*

GIRLS

ACTION CARDS

17 Is it God's will that I sometimes doubt him?
—*Read Mark 9:17-29; then take a Prayer Card and do what it says as a group.*

20 Is it God's will that disasters such as floods, storms and crashes happen?
—*Read Jeremiah 29:11. Then as a group, write the answer to the question on paper.*

21 Draw an Action Card and do what it says as a group.

22 Is it God's will that I be happy?
—*Read James 1:2-5; then take an Action Card and do what it says as a group.*

23 Is it God's will that I feel lonely sometimes?
—*Read Psalm 38:21-22; then take a Prayer Card and do what it says as a group.*

18 Is it God's will that I'm scared of what others think of me?
—*Read Matthew 10:26-33; then take an Action Card and do what it says as a group.*

19 Is it God's will that I look the way I do?
—*Read Psalm 139:13-14; then take an Action Card and do what it says as a group.* **14**

FINISH

24 Is it God's will for me to always obey my parents?
—*Read Ephesians 6:1-4; then take an Action Card and do what it says as a group.*

13 Draw an Action Card and do what it says as a group.

15 Is it God's will that I feel lonely sometimes?
—*Read Psalm 38:20-22; then take a Prayer Card and do what it says as a group.*

23 Was it God's will that a friend of mine died?
—*Read Hebrews 2:14-15; then take an Action Card and do what it says as a group.*

12 Is it God's will for my friends to have more things than me?
—*Read Hebrews 13:5-6. Then as a group, write the answer to the question on paper.*

16 Is it God's will that I worry about what others think of me?
—*Read Matthew 10:26-33; then take an Action Card and do what it says as a group.*

22 Is it God's will for me to fight back when others put me down?
—*Read Matthew 5:38-48; then take a Prayer Card and do what it says as a group.*

17 Is it God's will that I work for my allowance?
—*Read 2 Thessalonians 3:7-12. Then as a group, write the answer to the question on paper.*

11 Is it God's will that disasters such as floods, storms and crashes happen?
—*Read Jeremiah 29:11. Then as a group, write the answer to the question on paper.*

18 Is it God's will for my team to win?
—*Read Acts 10:34. Then as a group, write the answer to the question on paper.*

19 Is it God's will that people get a divorce?
—*Read 1 Corinthians 7:10-17; then take a Prayer Card and do what it says as a group.*

20 Draw an Action Card and do what it says as a group.

21 Is it God's will that I sometimes doubt him?
—*Read Mark 9:17-29; then take a Prayer Card and do what it says as a group.*

17 *Jesus Power*

By Ron Jensen

According to a Louis Harris poll, 75 percent of American adults think the problems teenagers face today are much greater than the problems they themselves faced as teenagers. But there was a generation of kids that lived in a more stressful time than today. Nineteen hundred years ago, young Christians and their parents believed Jesus would return any day. But days, months and years passed without a sign of his Return.

Those early Christians also had a more immediate problem—they lived in a society with priorities radically different from their own (sound familiar?). They were savagely persecuted. Some were killed. The young church needed reassurance. It needed to know God was in control of its out-of-control world. And God answered.

Imprisoned on the isle of Patmos, John received God's Revelation of things to come. God's message to his people was straightforward: ''I am a powerful God; my timing is perfect; I'm still in control of the world.'' John's Revelation from God was comforting to those early Christians. And it offers comfort to today's young believers as well. Use this meeting to introduce kids to God's care and protection.

OBJECTIVES

Participants will:

● learn to trust God because of who he is;

● understand the imagery used to describe the attributes of Jesus found in Revelation;

● learn how Jesus can be trusted to take care of them, even in an out-of-control world; and

● take home a personalized promise of Jesus' control over their circumstances and future.

BEFORE THE MEETING

Read the meeting, collect supplies and photocopy handouts.

Make name tags for activity #1: On 3×5 cards, write the names of famous people who have varying degrees of trustworthiness. For example, you could write the name of a religious figure, an actor or actress, or a rock star.

Photocopy and cut out the strips on the "Zoo Review" handout for activity #4.

THE MEETING

1. *Who can you trust?*—(For each person you'll need a famous-person name tag, tape and a Bible.) After kids arrive, tape a famous-person name tag to the back of each person and say: **Each of you has the name of a famous person taped to your back. That's your name tag, and the goal of this game is to find out your name by asking others in the room yes-and-no questions about that name. For example, you could ask "Am I living or dead?" or "Am I famous everywhere in the world?"**

When all the names have been guessed, ask kids to vote on the one person (from the name tags) they think is most trustworthy.

Ask:

● **Why is the person you chose more trustworthy than the others?**

Read aloud Matthew 21:28-32. Ask:

● **What makes a person trustworthy—what that person says or the kind of person he or she is? For example, do you trust people more because they say they're honest or because you've seen their honesty in action? Explain.**

2. *Crazy love notes*—(You'll need paper, markers and a Bible.) Say: **During the rest of the meeting, we're going to study a description of Jesus found in the book of Revelation. We'll find out how trustworthy he is to handle the circumstances we face every day. This description was written using some unusual imagery. To understand this imagery, we'll play a game using another image-filled scripture passage.**

Give kids each a piece of paper and some markers. Say: **As I read the following description of a woman, draw a picture of her just the way she's described** (for example, for verse 1 they should draw a woman's head with doves for eyes). Read aloud Song of Songs 4:1-4.

Have kids hold up their finished pictures. Ask:

● **Is this really the way this woman looked? Why or why not?**

● **Why did Solomon choose these words to describe his beloved?**

● **Can you think of words we use to describe others that shouldn't be taken literally (honey, devil, Ace)?**

3. *Unlocking a vision*—(You'll need an "Unlocking a Vision" handout for each person, Bibles, newsprint, a marker and pencils.) Have volunteers read aloud Revelation 1:9-20. Give each person an "Unlocking a Vision" handout and a pencil and say: **The left column lists part of John's vision of Jesus along with an explanation where necessary. The right column lists the possible meanings of the descriptions in the left column.**

Have kids complete the handout.

The answers to the handout are A-6, B-5, C-1, D-3, E-2 and F-4. Tape a sheet of newsprint on a wall. Have kids brainstorm other possible meanings for each descriptive phrase. Write their ideas on newsprint. At the bottom of the newsprint, write the numbers 1 through 5. Ask kids to call out five reasons Jesus is trustworthy. List the reasons after the numbers.

4. *God's Own Zoo*—(You'll need newsprint, a marker and a cloth flag. For each person you'll need an animal strip from the "Zoo Review" handout.) Form two teams. Have the teams line up across from each other against opposite walls in the room. Place a flag in the center of the room. Assign kids from each team a name taken from the "Zoo Review" handout. One young person

*Unlocking a Vision**

Instructions: Read the description in the left column from Revelation 1, then match it to its meaning in the right column by drawing a line connecting the two.

It looks like this in the Word:

**A. Jesus' Location
"among the lampstands" (v. 13)**
The lampstands are symbols of the churches (v. 20). So Jesus is walking among Christians.

**B. Jesus' Hair
"white like wool, as white as snow" (v. 14)**

**C. Jesus' Eyes
"were like blazing fire" (v. 14)**

**D. Jesus' Voice
"thundered like the waves against the shore" (v. 15)**

**E. Jesus' Right Hand
"held seven stars" (v. 16)**
The "stars" could symbolize messengers or angels, but probably are symbols for the "spirit" or general character of the individual churches. The right hand is the hand of favor (see Matthew 26:64).

**F. Jesus' Tongue
"out of his mouth came a sharp double-edged sword" (v. 16)**
The Roman military sword was shaped like a tongue.

It means Jesus is like this:

1. Keen; nothing misses Jesus' watchfulness.

2. Jesus dearly loves and protects those who follow him.

3. Jesus' words are powerful.

4. Jesus' words have authority.

5. Jesus is the "ancient of days." He has great wisdom.

6. Jesus never leaves us. He is closely involved in our lives.

*The information is taken from *The Revelation of St. John* by Leon Morris, part of the Tyndale New Testament Commentary series.

from each team should have the same name (for example, David from team #1 and Jennifer from team #2 are named "Lion"). If you have more than 10 kids, use names such as "Hawk 1," "Hawk 2" and so on.

Say: **When I call out a name, the one person from each team that has that name should run to the middle and try to capture the flag. The goal is either to grab the flag and run back to your team without getting tagged by your opponent, or wait for the other person to grab the flag and tag that person before he or she makes it back to the opposing team's wall. Only the people in the middle may chase each other. You'll get one point if you make it back to your team with the flag or if you tag your opponent when he or she has the flag.**

Make sure you pay attention, because I may call out two names at once sometimes.

After the game, form a circle and pass out the animal strips from the "Zoo Review" handout. Give the Hawk strip to one of the "Hawk" players, and so on with the other strips. Then have kids read aloud the strips one by one and discuss the following questions after each reading:

The Hawk—Read aloud Psalm 139. Ask:

● **How is God's sight like a hawk's?**

● **Are you comforted by God's ability to see you just as you are? challenged? both? Why or why not?**

● **How is God's watchfulness over you different from that of a prison guard?**

The Bear—Say: **The mother bear protects her cubs out of instinct. Why does God protect us?**

Read aloud Romans 8:32-39. Ask:

● **What are some things in your life that try to separate you from God's love?**

● **How has God protected you from harm in the past?**

Read aloud Psalm 23:4. Ask:

● **What's one reason we don't have to fear things that happen in the world?**

The Lion—Ask:

● **Why are lions called "the king of the beasts"? How is God like a lion?**

Read aloud Isaiah 40:10-26. Ask:

● **Can God be both gentle and fierce at the same**

Zoo Review

Instructions: Photocopy and cut apart these animal strips.

LION

An adult lion can eat up to 40 pounds of meat at a single sitting. Its powerful roar can be heard more than five miles away. It's no wonder this stately animal has earned the name "king of the beasts."

HAWK

An osprey, a member of the hawk family, can see a distant object eight times better than a person can. This bird can spot a fish from 200 feet in the air.

FOX

A fox has a reputation for being "wise," or at least crafty when pursued by hunters. In one instance, a pair of foxes exhausted a pack of dogs by taking turns running a one-mile circle, switching places in a hollow log. The dogs thought they were chasing one fox, not two!

BEAR

A bear can be large (one polar bear was 11 feet tall and weighed more than 2,000 pounds) and yet it can be fast (a large brown bear can reach speeds of 35 mph). Add to this the mother bear's strong protective instincts, and it's easy to see why it's so dangerous to come between a mamma bear and her cubs.

GOOSE

A Canada goose mates for life. And it's committed. If one goose is injured, the other will stay with it until it's healed. If a partner is lost, the other will continue searching through the deadly cold of winter.

128

time? Why or why not?
● Does God fear anyone or anything? Why or why not?
● How can you receive God's protective power?

The Fox—Say: **The fox uses its wisdom to stay alive.**
Ask:
● What does God use his wisdom for?
Read aloud Romans 11:33-36. Ask:
● Do we have to understand God's decisions to know whether or not they're good? Why or why not?
● Is God so wise that it's impossible to really know him? Why or why not?

The Goose—Ask:
● How are geese like human beings? like God?
Read aloud Joshua 1:5. Ask:
● Is God still committed to you even when you make a mistake or sin against him? Why or why not?
● How did Jesus prove he was committed to you?

5. A personal promise—(You'll need a "Personal Promise" handout and a pencil for each person.) Have kids each write their name in the blanks on the "Personal Promise" handout. Read the promise together; then have kids take it home as a reminder of God's love and protection.

Personal Promise

"_____, don't be afraid. I existed before the first person was created and I'll be here after the last person is gone from the Earth. I am forever, the Living One. I was dead, but now look! I'm alive forever! I have control over circumstances, even over death and hell itself.

"_____, if I control all this, you can be sure that I have control over everything that concerns you. Be patient, remember my great power and know that together with you, I'm working out all the smallest details of your future."

All my love,
Jesus

(A personalized version of Revelation 1:17-18.)

18 Ups and Downs of Faith

By Dennis Becker

Junior highers, like all of us, have ups and downs in their faith. But since junior highers lack the life experience to put their ups and downs in proper perspective, they may question themselves, their faith and God.

You can reassure junior highers that faith is a process—for everyone. Even Elijah, a great prophet in Bible times, had high points and low points in his walk with God.

Use this meeting to help junior highers see how their ups and downs are similar to those experienced by Elijah and how they can find help in their faith just like Elijah did.

OBJECTIVES

Participants will:
- hear and "experience" some stories from Elijah's life;
- discover how they face situations similar to those Elijah faced;
- compare Elijah's ups and downs in faith with their own; and
- learn how they can strengthen their faith in the same ways Elijah did.

130

BEFORE THE MEETING

Read the meeting, collect supplies and photocopy handouts. Ask group members each to bring a flashlight.

For activity #2, you'll need two loaded water pistols. You'll also need a large platter of cookies and a glass of juice for each person.

Practice telling Elijah's story from 1 Kings 16:29—19:18. Or find a congregation member who's a good storyteller and have him or her prepare to tell the story.

THE MEETING

1. *Welcome*—Greet kids as they arrive. Tell kids this meeting is about faith—and you're going to begin with a story about Elijah. Get everyone in a circle.

2. *Elijah's story*—(You'll need two copies of the "Elijah's Story in Action" sheet, the flashlights and the loaded water pistols.) Recruit two kids to lead the group in the actions for Elijah's story. Give them both an "Elijah's Story in Action" sheet to tell them what to do. Set the flashlights and loaded water pistols nearby. Tell the story of Elijah from 1 Kings 16:29—19:18, or have a congregation member tell the story. Enjoy watching group members act out the story!

3. *Me? Like Elijah?*—Get kids back in a circle. Have a group member read James 5:17. Highlight the phrase, "Elijah was a man just like us." Say: **We have the same kinds of problems: having to confront someone who's doing something wrong; choosing between right and wrong; worrying about food, clothes and other material things; feeling depressed and lonely. And just as Elijah got help from God, so can we.**

4. *Tough experiences*—(You'll need newsprint and a marker. For each group of four to six, you'll need an "Elijah Experience Card" and a Bible.) Say: **Elijah faced some tough experiences, just like you do. Let's look at Elijah's experiences and see how he got help.**

Form groups of four to six, with an adult sponsor in each. Give each group an "Elijah Experience Card" and a Bible. Have each group follow the instructions on the card.

Elijah's Story in Action

Leader tells about these sections	Kids do these actions	
1 Kings 16:29—17:1: Elijah confronts Ahab about worshiping Baal and says it will not rain unless he (Elijah) says it will.	Shake fingers at each other and whisper "Naughty! Naughty!"	
1 Kings 17:2-6: God tells Elijah to go away to a brook; there, ravens bring Elijah food.	Flap arms and "fly" around the meeting area.	
1 Kings 17:7-24: God tells Elijah to stay with a widow, and her supply of food doesn't run out.	Eat cookies and drink juice.	
1 Kings 18:1-15: Elijah and Obadiah meet unexpectedly; Elijah tells Obadiah to tell Ahab he (Elijah) is back.	Walk around the room in pairs, with arms linked.	
1 Kings 18:16-40: Elijah challenges Ahab's prophets of Baal on Mount Carmel; Baal doesn't respond, but God sends fire for the altar.	Turn on flashlights for God's fire from heaven. And when leader finishes telling the story, shout "Is Baal asleep? Is Baal on a trip? Ha!"	
1 Kings 18:41-46: Elijah prays for rain and God sends a downpour.	Two leaders squirt water pistols at everyone.	
1 Kings 19:1-18: Elijah becomes depressed, lonely and afraid and flees to Horeb, where God talks with him.	Sit with heads between their knees.	

132

Elijah Experience Cards

Elijah Confronts Ahab

Read 1 Kings 16:29—17:1 and answer these questions.
1. What situation did Elijah face?
2. How do you think Elijah felt?
3. What did Elijah do?
4. What gave Elijah strength to act?
Discuss: What would you do if you knew your best friends were cheating on tests?

Elijah Is Alone With God

Read 1 Kings 17:2-6 and 18:41-46 and answer these questions.
1. What situation did Elijah face?
2. How do you think Elijah felt?
3. What did Elijah do?
4. What gave Elijah strength to act?
Discuss: What would you do if you wanted to strengthen your relationship with God?

Elijah Confronts the Prophets of Baal

Read 1 Kings 18:16-40 and answer these questions.
1. What situation did Elijah face?
2. How do you think Elijah felt?
3. What did Elijah do?
4. What gave Elijah strength to act?
Discuss: All the popular kids in school smoke marijuana. One of them offers you a joint. You'd like to be a part of the popular group. What would you do?

Elijah Fears for His Life

Read 1 Kings 19:1-18 and answer these questions.
1. What situation did Elijah face?
2. How do you think Elijah felt?
3. What did Elijah do?
4. What gave Elijah strength to act?
Discuss: You're depressed. You feel like nobody cares whether you live or die. You think you're not good enough for even God to care about. What would you do?

After the groups finish the assignments, have kids get back in a circle. Ask kids to tell what Elijah did to get help, or what helped Elijah through his tough experiences. List their answers on newsprint. If kids don't name these, add and discuss:

- Elijah had faith in a living God (1 Kings 17:1);
- Elijah knew he served God (1 Kings 17:1);
- Elijah believed God's promises (1 Kings 17:4-5);
- Elijah believed that God was stronger than Baal (1 Kings 18:24);
- Elijah prayed (1 Kings 18:36, 42);
- Elijah took care of his physical needs (1 Kings 19:6);
- Elijah talked about his feelings (1 Kings 19:14);
- Elijah slowed down to wait for God (1 Kings 19:11-12); and
- Elijah realized he wasn't alone (1 Kings 19:18).

5. *Ups and downs*—Say: **Even though Elijah did all of this, his faith went up and down. He didn't always appear to have a strong faith. Our faith goes up and down just like Elijah's. We may not always look like strong Christians.**

Have kids rate Elijah's levels of faith during certain experiences. Demonstrate these positions:

- stand on tiptoe and hold their hands high above their heads to indicate a very high faith level;
- stand with arms at their sides to indicate a high faith level;
- stand with the top half of their bodies bent over to indicate an average faith level;
- sit down to indicate a low faith level; and
- lie down flat on their backs to indicate a very low faith level.

Have kids practice so they'll easily remember them. Call out these times in Elijah's life, allowing time for kids to get in their faith-level positions:

- **confronting Ahab;**
- **going to the brook for food and water;**
- **being alone with God;**
- **confronting the prophets of Baal;**
- **praying for rain; and**
- **fearing for his life.**

Say: **Now, let's see how our faith may go up and down, just like Elijah's. Use the same rating positions for your faith level in these experiences:**

● **confronting a friend about a problem;**
● **wondering what would happen if your dad lost his job;**
● **feeling lonely and afraid;**
● **choosing whether to do something you know is wrong; and**
● **being alone with God.**

6. *Switching on help*—(You'll need the list you created earlier of ways Elijah got help. For each person, you'll need a flashlight.) Call group members' attention to the list of ways Elijah got help and what things helped him. Say: **When you get help in a tough situation, everything seems brighter.**

Give each person a flashlight. Tell kids you're going to read statements about ways Elijah found help, but make the statements apply to the kids' lives. Have kids walk around. Tell them to think about whether each statement is true for them. If it's true, they should switch on their flashlights to show that's one way they find help. After a few seconds they should switch off their flashlights and wait for you to read the next statement.

Turn out the lights. With a flashlight of your own, read aloud these statements. Add others suggested from your newsprint list.

1. I think about my faith in a living God.

2. I know I want to serve God.

3. I believe the promises of God.

4. I know God is stronger than Satan.

5. I pray about my problems and thank God for answers to prayer.

6. I get enough rest and nourishing food.

7. I talk about my feelings.

8. I slow down and wait for God when I'm confused about what to do.

9. I talk to my Christian friends about decisions I have to make.

7. *Prayer*—Keep the lights off. Have group members turn off and put down their flashlights, hold hands and form a circle. You stand near the light switch. Have group members say sentence prayers of thanksgiving for the strength God gives to their faith. When the last person has prayed, have kids say ''Amen'' together. Turn on the light.

19 What to Do When God Says No

By Rick Bundschuh

Most junior highers have an understandably simple prayer life. Often, their prayers are the "help get me outta trouble" variety. They want something that God has. But if God granted the requests of all those who prayed in this way, we'd be surprised and disappointed at some of the results.

Use this meeting to encourage kids into a deeper understanding of God and prayer. Stimulate your kids' desire to pray and share their hearts with God.

OBJECTIVES

Participants will:
- complete a cartoon strip and discover that it's not always good to get what they want;
- explore different aspects of prayer through five creative projects;
- find out about Bible characters who prayed but were denied their requests; and
- write prayers that they'll look at later and see how God answered.

BEFORE THE MEETING

Read the meeting, collect supplies and photocopy handouts. Complete the "When God Says No" handout so you'll know the answers.

136

THE MEETING

1. *Cartoon completion*—(For each person you'll need a copy of the "Just Say No" cartoon and a pencil.) Give kids each a "Just Say No" cartoon and ask them each to complete the story by drawing the final two panels of the cartoon.

When kids are finished, form groups of two or more. Say: **Explain your cartoon to the other members of your group.**

After kids talk about their cartoons, ask:

● **Should you always get what you want? Why or why not?**

● **Is it less or more loving for your parents to give you what you want all the time? Explain.**

● **How would you feel if you were the parent in the cartoon?**

● **How would you feel if you were the young person?**

● **If parents say no to a request, should they always give an explanation? Why or why not?**

Say: **Sometimes we ask God for something we're sure we need. But God—because he's a good parent and has a better perspective than our own, sometimes says no. And it's hard for us to understand why our prayers are denied. God can seem cruel because he won't give us what we want. But he always has good reasons for saying no.**

2. *Prayer stew*—(You'll need construction paper, scissors, tape and a cooking pot. For each person you'll need at least one "Prayer Stew Card," a marker and a pencil.) Put the "Prayer Stew Cards" in a cooking pot and place it with construction paper, scissors and tape in a central location. Form pairs and have each person pick a card from the container. Tell partners to complete the exercises on both of their cards using the supplies provided. If some kids finish before others, ask them to choose another "Prayer Stew Card" and complete the activity.

Have kids who completed "Card #1—Prayer Traffic Signs" tape their signs on the meeting room walls. Have kids who completed "Card #2—Kids' Prayer" read their prayers aloud to the group. Have kids who completed "Card #3—Prayer Cartoon" tape their cartoons on the meeting room walls. Have kids who completed "Card #4—Prayer Bumper Sticker" tape their bumper stickers on the meeting room walls. Have kids who completed "Card #5—Prayer Jingle" sing their songs to the group. Have kids

Prayer Stew Cards

Card #1—Prayer Traffic Signs

Read Matthew 6:5-8. Create several new traffic signs out of construction paper that represent the warnings about ineffective prayer Jesus mentions in this passage. Look below for examples of the shapes and messages you see on traffic signs every day, then make up your own.

Card #2—Kids' Prayer

Suppose a 4-year-old asked you to teach him or her to pray. Read Matthew 6:7-15 and rewrite this famous passage in language so simple that a little kid could understand it.

_____
_____
_____
_____
_____
_____
_____
_____

Card #3—Prayer Cartoon

Read Luke 11:5-10 and create a cartoon strip showing what happens in this parable. At the end of your cartoon strip, explain what you think Jesus meant by this story.

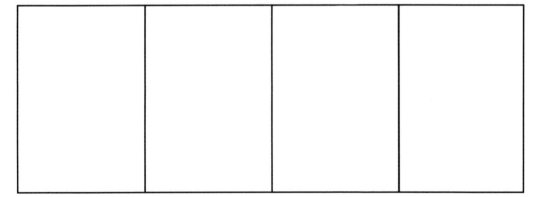

continued

138

Card #4—Prayer Bumper Sticker

Read 2 Chronicles 7:14 and create a bumper sticker or slogan that expresses the idea behind this passage of scripture. Look below for an example.

Humble Prayer Heals

Card #5—Prayer Jingle

Read Mark 11:25 and describe what Jesus is saying using new words set to a popular tune. Some examples of tunes you could use: "Rudolph the Red Nosed Reindeer," "Amazing Grace" and "Pass It On" (or think of your own tune).

_____

_____

_____

_____

_____

---

circulate around the room and look at the projects taped on the walls.

3. *When God says no*—(For each person you'll need a "When God Says No" handout and a pencil.) Give each person a "When God Says No" handout.

Say: **Complete your handout, then we'll go through it together.**

After kids finish their handouts and you check their answers, ask:

● **Do you think God listens to the prayers of a wicked person?**

● **What are some reasons God might say no to our prayers?**

● **Can you think of a time you asked for something but had to wait before you got an answer?**

● **Why is waiting sometimes better than getting what you want right away?**

● **Why don't people who are sincere and pray with great faith always get what they ask for?**

● **Is it better to ask God for the desires of your heart or ask him to change what your heart desires? Explain.**

When God Says No

Instructions: Read each scripture passage and draw a line between the person and the request denied.

David (2 Samuel 12:15-20)   Prayed to "let this cup pass . . ."

Paul (2 Corinthians 12:7-9)   Asked to cross the Jordan River but was only allowed to see the Promised Land.

Mary (and Martha) (John 11:1-46)   Pleaded with God to spare the life of his child.

Jesus (Matthew 26:39, 42, 44)   Asked that the thorn in his flesh be removed.

Moses (Deuteronomy 3:23-27)   Asked Jesus to heal Lazarus.

140

4. Closing—(You'll need a large manila envelope. For each person you'll need a pencil, a piece of paper and an envelope.) Have kids each write three personal prayers on a piece of paper, fold it, place it in an envelope and write their name on the front. Collect the envelopes and seal them in a large manila envelope. Keep the envelope sealed for a month, then open it and hand back the prayer requests to kids. At that time, tape a large sheet of newsprint on a wall with the following three headings written on the top: "Yes," "No" and "Still Waiting." Ask kids how many "Yes," "No" and "Still Waiting" answers they received. Mark their answers under the appropriate headings.

Close by forming a circle and asking kids to think of their three prayer requests. Say: **Imagine you're personally bringing your requests to the house where Jesus is staying in Jerusalem. As you enter the door and approach Jesus to tell him your prayers, what does his face look like?**

Have kids, one by one, say one word that describes Jesus' face. Then have kids each thank him for his love and faithfulness.

Just Say No

Section Five:

ISSUES

20 Facing Death

By Steven McCullough

For most junior highers, death is a distant, insignificant event. But when it happens to someone close to them, death becomes an outrage, says Dan Toomey, head of Evanston Hospital's Good Grief program in Illinois. The reason, he says, is that adolescents "feel invincible." They've seen so many killings on television—where no consequences are shown—that death becomes "no big deal."

Use this meeting to get your junior highers talking about death. Help them see death from God's perspective and learn how to deal with it.

OBJECTIVES

Participants will:
- confront their feelings about death;
- recognize that it's okay to have questions about death; and
- learn to turn to Christ when they're forced to deal with death.

BEFORE THE MEETING

Read the meeting, collect supplies and photocopy handouts.

For activity #1, prepare healthy snacks or small trinkets to give as prizes.

For activity #2, ask a pet shop if you may have a small, dead animal (such as a hamster or a bird) to show kids. Don't use someone's pet or something that's offensive. As a last resort, bring a stuffed animal. Bring a box to use as a coffin, locate a place you can bury the animal and bring a shovel to dig with.

For activity #3, draw a large chart (about five feet long) on newsprint that looks similar to:

Death's Doorways

Scripture	Type of Death		
Why does it happen?	Suicide	Old age or disease	Accidents
● Genesis 3			
● Genesis 4			
● Luke 13:1-9			

Depending upon the time you have available, hold the meeting at a mortuary or a cemetery.

THE MEETING

1. *Omega*—(You'll need healthy snacks or small trinkets to give as prizes.) Greet kids as they arrive as if you're welcoming them to a funeral. In somber tones, say, "Thank you for coming . . . I know this is a difficult time."

Gather everyone together and say: **Today we're going to talk about death. And throughout the meeting, we'll play a game called Omega. Whenever I call out "Omega!" that means everyone should drop to the floor and lie stiff and quiet until I call out "Omega!" again. The person who "plays dead" the best each time will receive a small prize.**

Each time you call out "Omega!," extend the time from 30 to 60 to 90 to 120 seconds. Play the game three or four times throughout the meeting. Award a prize each time.

Call out "Omega!" While the participants are lying still, say: **It's pretty easy to lie still for short periods of time. But** could you do the same thing forever? Is this what death will be like?

Read aloud Luke 16:19-31. Say: **It's good to think about death now while we're alive because there's nothing we can do to change our attitudes or actions after we're dead.**

2. *The solemn ceremony*—(You'll need a small, dead animal or a stuffed animal and a shoe box decorated to look like a coffin. You'll also need a "gravesite" and a shovel to dig with.) Ask for two volunteers. Bring out your "coffin" with the dead animal in it.

Say: **You're all participants in the funeral of the late, great (name of animal). I've already picked out a gravesite, so follow our two volunteer "pall bearers" and me to the spot.**

Have the two volunteers carry the shoe box to the gravesite. Once everyone is gathered around the gravesite, give a eulogy for the deceased. Say something about the animal's past, its impact on the world, the family it left behind, and the memories that will live on. Then have each person take a turn digging the grave. Meanwhile, have two volunteers find something in the area to serve as a grave marker. Put the "coffin" in the hole and cover it with dirt.

Observe a moment of silence for the deceased, then say: **Death affects all of us. It's as much a part of life as birth. Most people don't like to talk about death because they're afraid of it. But God has taken the sting of death away for those who follow him.**

Read aloud Isaiah 25:8-9. Say: **If you know someone who's died, tell us how you felt when it happened.**

After a few people share their experiences, return to the meeting place.

3. *Death's doorways*—(You'll need a "Death's Doorways" chart printed on newsprint, and for every three people you'll need a marker, a Bible, a newspaper, scissors and glue.) Form groups of three. Give each group a newspaper, scissors and glue.

Point out the "Death's Doorways" chart and say: **Death can come in many different ways. Look through your newspaper and cut out every article or reference to death. Then glue that article or reference to the "Death's Doorways" chart in the appropriate place.**

After kids have glued their articles to the chart, assign each group one of the scripture passages listed on the chart. Give each group a marker and a Bible.

Say: **Read your scripture passage, then answer the question on the chart for one of the three kinds of death. Write your group's answer under the appropriate category.**

4. *Bounce Around*—(You'll need a "The Truth About Death" handout, a pencil and a Bible for every three people.) Say: **We're going to play a game called Bounce Around. The object is to jump up and down continuously until you can't jump anymore. When you stop jumping, you're "dead," and you must lie down right where you are. The last one jumping wins.**

Tell kids to start bouncing, then declare a winner. Say: **You played dead when you couldn't jump anymore. But you quickly recovered from your "death." When life ends for real, your body won't recover.**

Form teams of three and give each team a "The Truth About Death" handout, a pencil and a Bible. Say: **In your team, fill in the blanks on your handout with the correct words. Read the scriptures listed for help. The first team to finish will receive two bonus points. Otherwise, your team will receive one point for every correct answer. The team with the most points wins.**

Gather together and have groups share how they filled in the blanks on their handouts. Then give the answers.

Ask:
● **Is it right for Christians to grieve and cry when people they know die? Why or why not?**
● **Do you think Jesus was afraid to die? Why or why not?**
● **Which would be harder for you—facing death yourself or facing the death of someone close to you? Explain.**

5. *Breathless*—(For each person you'll need a balloon and a marker.) Have kids stay in their teams of three. Say: **Let's see who can hold their breath the longest. On "go," hold your breath. The person on each team who can hold his or her breath the longest will compete against the winners from the other teams. The winner of the second round is declared the "Breathless" champion.**

146

The Truth About Death

Instructions: Fill in the blanks with the correct word or words.

1. Because all of us have _____, all of us deserve death (Romans 6:23).

2. Jesus told his disciples they should not let their hearts be _____ _____ about death because he was going to prepare a _____ for them (John 14:1-2).

3. Once we die, how will we know how to get to God's kingdom? Jesus said we would know the way because the path was through_____ (John 14:6).

4. We have hope that we'll have contact with those who have died before us because _____ (1 Thessalonians 4:16-17).

5. When Jesus returns to bring all his followers home to heaven, he'll take _____ first and then he'll gather all those who are _____ to follow after (1 Thessalonians 4:16-17).

6. According to the Bible, death will be swallowed up in_____ (1 Corinthians 15:54).

7. The sting of death is _____, and since Jesus has removed that sting if we follow him, we should always_____ _____ (1 Corinthians 14:56-58).

Say "Go," and determine the winners from each team. Then repeat the process for the second round. Declare an overall winner.

Say: **Notice how your body struggled to breathe while you were holding your breath. No matter how hard you tried, all of you had to breathe to keep from dying. Our bodies will eventually die, but not without a struggle. Death wasn't part of God's original plan. But since sin entered the world, all things eventually die. That's why Jesus came to give us life. If you accept and follow Jesus, your body will die but your spirit will live with him in heaven.**

Read aloud John 3:16-17. Then give kids each a balloon and a marker. Say: **Blow up your balloon and tie it off. Now you've captured the breath that symbolizes your life. On your balloon, write three things that give you hope as you think about death. Then take your balloon home as a reminder of God's promises to you.**

The Truth About Death

Answer Key

1. sinned
2. troubled; place
3. him
4. the dead in Christ will be raised first, and those remaining alive in Christ will join them in the air to meet the Lord Jesus
5. the dead in Christ; still alive
6. victory
7. sin; be giving ourselves fully to the work of the Lord, because we know that our labor in the Lord is not in vain

21 *Jesus vs. Rambo*

By Ed McNulty

The Bureau of Justice reports that every year one out of 15 teenagers is somehow involved in a violent crime. And 2.3 million violent crimes are attempted or committed by or against young people every year. A sobering 99 percent of kids will have something stolen from them by age 12.

Sometimes kids copycat the violent acts they see on television or in movies. Shortly after a violent sexual attack was shown in the NBC movie *Born Innocent*, a young girl was assaulted in a similar way.

Today kids are exposed to so much violence that many psychologists believe they've become desensitized to it. Some kids grow up learning that violence is the accepted response to all kinds of problems and stresses.

Use this meeting to help your kids understand the influence of violence and choose to follow the Prince of Peace.

OBJECTIVES

Participants will:

● learn to recognize the violent messages they receive through the media;

- discover violent tendencies they might have;
- compare how Jesus and Rambo respond to violence;
- make a collage of images representing God's view of violence and people's view of violence; and
- take one practical action to curb violence in their lives.

BEFORE THE MEETING

Read the meeting, collect supplies and photocopy handouts.

Set up a VCR and television in your meeting room. Rent a popular PG-rated action movie or check your TV listings for an action show that airs during your meeting. (Note: If you choose to rent a movie, be sure you secure permission from the distributor to show it to a group.)

Write "Smash 'Em" and "Hug 'Em" on separate sheets of newsprint. Tape the sheets on opposite ends of a wall.

Find a newspaper with articles on violence and write in bold, red letters at the top "For God so loved . . ." Tape the newspaper on a wall.

THE MEETING

1. *Video violence*—(You'll need a television. If you choose the movie option, you'll also need a rented movie and a VCR. For each person you'll need paper, a pencil, a Bible and a "Blessed Are They?" handout.) When kids arrive, give each paper and a pencil. Say: **In this meeting, we'll talk about violence and its effect on your life. We'll look at the violence in our society. And we'll learn God's response to violence. To start, I'm going to play five minutes of television (or a rented movie). Every time you see an act of violence, make a mark on your paper. We'll see how sensitive each of you is to the violence you see during this time.**

Play the video or television for five minutes. Ask kids to total and compare their marks. Ask those with the highest totals:

- **Do you think you're particularly sensitive to violence? Why or why not?**
- **Are you uncomfortable watching violent movies or TV shows? Why or why not?**

Ask those with the lowest totals:

- **Do you rarely notice violent acts? Why or why not?**
- **Do you enjoy watching violence, or does it make you feel uncomfortable? Explain.**

150

Give each person a "Blessed Are They?" handout and a Bible. Say: **Look up the Bible verses on your handout, read Jesus' words, then fill in the blanks on your handout with words that Rambo would use. For example, Matthew 5:3 could be reworded to read: "Blessed are the strong in spirit, for theirs is the kingdom of heaven."**

After kids each finish their handout, ask:

● **How is Jesus' philosophy of life different from Rambo's?**

● **If you had a choice to live under either Rambo's or Jesus' authority, which would you choose? Explain.**

2. *Peace or punches?*—(For each person you'll need a "Peace or Punches?" handout and a pencil.) Give each person a "Peace or Punches?" handout and a pencil. Ask kids each to respond to the statements by circling true or false.

After kids each fill out their handout, go over each statement and discuss kids' answers.

3. *Smash 'em or hug 'em*—(You'll need the "Smash 'Em" and "Hug 'Em" signs posted at either end of a wall, and you'll need a Bible for each person.) Say: **After you hear each statement, move toward the sign with the reaction you'd most likely give. The closer you place yourself to either sign, the stronger your reaction.**

After you read a statement from the "Smash 'Em or Hug 'Em?" box and kids move somewhere on the continuum, ask kids from both extremes to explain their positions.

Read aloud Romans 12:9-21. Ask:

● **How does the passage say we should respond to violence?**

● **According to the passage, how should we treat our enemies?**

● **If God is the father of all people, what does that make our enemies?**

● **Is it possible to live the way Paul says we should live? Why or why not?**

4. *The media tells the story*—(You'll need a stack of newspapers and magazines, and for every three people you'll need a Bible, a piece of posterboard, markers, glue and scissors.) Read aloud Genesis 4:23-24 and Micah 4:3-4; then explain the passages' contrasting views of violence. Form groups of three, as-

Blessed Are They?

Instructions: Read Matthew 5:1-12, 38-39, 43-44. If Rambo, instead of Jesus, spoke to the people on the mountain, what would he say? Fill in the blanks with words you think Rambo would say.

● "Blessed are the _____, for they will inherit the earth."

● "Blessed are those who _____, for they will be filled."

● "Blessed are the _____makers, for they will be called sons of _____."

● "If someone strikes you on the right cheek, _____."

● "_____ your enemies."

Permission to photocopy this handout granted for local church use. Copyright © 1989 by Thom Schultz Publications, Inc., Box 481, Loveland, CO 80539.

Peace or Punches?

Instructions: For each statement, circle true or false.

Statement

1. I'd rather play King of the Hill than Charades.	True	False
2. I'd rather see *Rambo III* than *The Sound of Music*.	True	False
3. I'd get a bigger thrill out of watching a hockey fight than a sunset.	True	False
4. I'd rather kick down a sand castle than build one.	True	False
5. I've seen at least three horror movies this year.	True	False
6. I can name three TV wrestlers.	True	False
7. I think that Rambo is a better example of manhood than Mr. Rogers.	True	False
8. I can think of someone I'd like to beat up if I could.	True	False

Permission to photocopy this handout granted for local church use. Copyright © 1989 by Thom Schultz Publications, Inc., Box 481, Loveland, CO 80539.

152

Smash 'Em or Hug 'Em?

1. A friend makes a nasty remark about you.
2. Someone you don't like makes the same nasty remark about you.
3. A friend insults your mom or dad.
4. Someone you don't like insults your mom or dad.
5. Someone you don't like picks a fight with you.
6. Someone bigger than you keeps teasing you.
7. Someone smaller than you keeps teasing you.
8. The President announces that he's sending troops into a Latin American country to fight communists.
9. Your school's team is beaten by a rival. In your opinion, the rival team got away with cheap shots during the game. After the game a gang of the other team's supporters taunts you and calls you chicken.
10. The school bully gets beaten up by a new kid.

sign one of the two scripture passages to each group, and give each group a stack of newspapers and magazines.

Say: **Read your assigned passage again and then look through the magazines and newspapers for pictures and words that reflect the meaning of that passage. Make a collage and give it a title.**

Gather together and have groups each explain their collage to the whole group.

yes

5. *What can I do?*—(For each person you'll need a "Prayer of St. Francis" handout, a 3×5 card, a pencil and glue.) Say: **There are no easy answers to the problem of violence. The Christian response to violence may well involve a cross, or some other suffering, just as it did for Jesus. Think of someone you consider an enemy. How would Rambo deal with that person? How would Jesus deal with that person?**

Give each person a 3×5 card and a "Prayer of St. Francis" handout. Together read it aloud. Have kids each glue the prayer to one side of a 3×5 card. On the other side, have them each write the name of the enemy they were thinking about and write one way they can react to that person the way Jesus would.

Prayer of St. Francis

Lord, make me an instrument of your peace:
where there is hatred . . . let me sow love;
where there is injury . . . pardon;
where there is doubt . . . faith;
where there is despair . . . hope;
where there is darkness . . . light;
where there is sadness . . . joy.

O Divine Master, grant that I may not so much seek
to be consoled . . . as to console;
not so much to be understood . . . as to understand;
not so much to be loved . . . as to love.

For it is in giving that we receive,
it is in pardoning that we are pardoned,
it is in dying that we awaken to eternal life.

22 Managing Your Moods

By Kurt Bickel

Like a child on a swing, a junior higher feels "up," "down," then "up" and "down" again . . . and so on. It's part of being a junior higher.

Junior highers are just beginning to experience many feelings—self-doubt, confidence, rebellion, depression, jubilation. Things are either "the best" or "the worst." You notice times when some of your kids are in a bad mood and don't want to do anything. Other times, the same kids are ready to take on the world.

Use this meeting to help kids learn to control how they react to feelings. Help kids learn coping skills and discuss feelings and moods in light of two biblical characters.

OBJECTIVES

Participants will:
- see how biblical characters dealt with feelings;
- share their feelings with others and with God;
- gain ideas for helping friends handle their emotions; and
- set goals for good ways to deal with mood swings.

BEFORE THE MEETING

Read the meeting, collect supplies and photocopy handouts. Choose two rooms to serve as mood rooms; one for a sad room and one for a happy room. Your meeting will take place in these two rooms. Ask kids to bring items from home to decorate the rooms and create the desired moods. For example, the sad room might have slow music, candlelight and pillow furniture; the happy room might have exciting posters, upbeat music, balloons, bright lights and colored streamers.

THE MEETING

1. *Set the mood*—(You'll need decorating supplies, two tape players, slow and upbeat music cassettes, candles, magazines, markers and scissors.) As kids arrive, have them help you get the two mood rooms ready, using your supplies and whatever they brought from home. Have kids use the magazines and markers to make mood posters for the rooms.

2. *Make my day*—Have kids arrange chairs in a circle in the happy room and have them sit in them. Read aloud each of the following statements, allowing time between each one for kids to move. Add more "If" statements if you like. Have fun!

● **If you've had a bad day this week, move two seats to the left.**

● **If you've laughed a lot this week, move one seat to the right.**

● **If you snapped at someone this week, move three seats to the right.**

● **If you've been depressed at all this week, move one seat to the left.**

● **If someone really got on your nerves this week, move three seats to the left.**

● **If you've been in a great mood all week, move five seats to the right.**

● **If you generally feel happier in the mornings than you do in the afternoons, move four seats to the left.**

● **If you're never depressed, move five seats to the left.**

3. *King vs. apostles*—(You'll need Bibles, a newsprint scoreboard and cheat sheets.) Form two teams (still in the happy room). Hand out Bibles. Give one team copies of the King David portion of the "Cheat Sheets" and the other copies of the Apostle Peter portion. Challenge the teams to "cram" and study these passages. Each team should divide the passages among its members for studying, then have individuals report.

Cheat Sheets

King David
- 1 Samuel 17:22-51 (David and Goliath)
- 2 Samuel 1:1-16 (David grieves for Saul and Jonathan)
- 2 Samuel 11:1-5, 14-17, 26-27 (David's sins)
- 2 Samuel 12:1-20 (David is punished)
- 2 Samuel 23:1-7 (David's last words)

✂ -

Apostle Peter
- Mark 1:14-18 (Peter is chosen)
- Matthew 14:22-32 (Peter walks on water)
- Mark 9:2-9 (Peter sees Christ transfigured)
- Luke 22:54-62 (Peter denies Jesus)
- John 21:15-19 (The resurrected Christ talks with Peter)

Inform the teams that they'll be asked questions about the story of each passage, how the character in the passage felt and what the passage means.

Have the scoreboard ready, and when the teams have studied their passages, announce that each round will have three questions per team. Hold as many rounds as time permits. The questions will have different point values. Each team will have 30 seconds to come up with the answer to its question. Each team must select a specific "answer person" to give the answer. The team with the most points at the end of the game wins. See page 157 for questions.

4. *Guided reflection*—Begin moving into the sad room. As you do, point out to kids the differences in the atmospheres of the two rooms. Say that a bleak environment, whether the bleakness is physical or emotional, can contribute to depression.

King David and Apostle Peter Questions

Round One
King David
1. (two points) Why did David learn to use a slingshot? (He learned to use a slingshot to protect his father's sheep.)
2. (three points) Why did David feel confident against Goliath? (David believed his God would give him victory.)
3. (five points) Can someone tell about a time you felt confident, and why?

Apostle Peter
1. (two points) Peter was not always Peter. Who did he used to be? (Simon.)
2. (three points) What did Jesus do to cause Peter to drop his fishing net and follow him? (He called Peter and Andrew to follow him, saying he would make them fishers of men.)
3. (five points) Can someone remember a time you were chosen last for a team? How did it feel?

Round Two
King David
1. (two points) How did Saul and Jonathan die? (They were killed during a battle.)
2. (three points) Name three things David did that showed his feelings. (Tore his clothes, wept and fasted.)
3. (five points) Name five feelings someone has when a loved one dies.

Apostle Peter
1. (two points) At what time did Jesus come walking on the lake? (Fourth watch, or between 3 and 6 a.m.)
2. (three points) Name three feelings Peter had the night Jesus walked on water. (Fear, courage, doubt.)
3. (five points) Can someone relate a time when you felt you were sinking in the sea of life?

Round Three
King David
1. (two points) David arranged to have one of his soldiers die in battle. Who and why? (Uriah, because David wanted to marry Uriah's wife, Bathsheba.)
2. (three points) Sometimes strong feelings make us ignore good behavior. How was that true for King David? (His desire for Bathsheba caused him to commit adultery and murder.)
3. (five points) Name four feelings that can lead us into bad behaviors.

Apostle Peter
1. (two points) What was Peter's mountaintop experience? (He saw Christ transfigured.)

2. (three points) Peter tried to express how wonderful this experience was. What did he say? (He said it was good for them to be there, and offered to build a shelter for Jesus and each of the men with him.)
3. (five points) After that incredible experience on the mountaintop, Jesus, Peter, James and John went down to the valley. Can anyone tell about a great, high mood you had that was followed by a deep, low mood?

Round Four
King David
1. (two points) Who came to David, and who sent him? (Nathan. God sent him.)
2. (three points) What was the story the prophet Nathan told David and how did David feel about it? (About the man who stole the lamb. David was furious.)
3. (five points) Name five ways sin can ruin relationships.

Apostle Peter
1. (two points) Peter wanted to not be noticed in the crowd. Where was he? (Peter was sitting by a fire in a courtyard.)
2. (three points) What made Peter remember Jesus' prediction that he would deny Jesus? (A rooster crowed and the Lord looked at Peter.)
3. (five points) Can someone share a time you felt betrayed, and a time you were the betrayer?

Round Five
King David
1. (two points) When David was old and looked back on his life, what did he do to explain his feelings? (He recited an oracle, or a poem.)
2. (three points) What four things did David say God had done for him? (He said God had spoken through him, had set up a covenant with him, had saved him and had given him his every desire.)
3. (five points) If you were writing a poem, what would you say God has done for you?

Apostle Peter
1. (two points) What did Jesus mean when he said, "Feed my sheep?" (To care for others.)
2. (three points) In what way is this story the same as the story of Peter's denial of Jesus? (Jesus gave Peter three chances to say he loved him.)
3. (five points) Can someone tell how you can feed Jesus' lambs?

Once everyone is in the sad room, have kids sit down. Tell them to each pick an object in the room, such as a candle or poster (but not a person), and focus their attention on that object. Ask kids to listen to your voice only and reflect on their moods.

Then read the following, pausing between sentences.

Say: **Please be quiet and listen carefully to me. Relax and be comfortable.**

I'm going to ask you to think about your moods. Take a deep breath and let it out slowly. Make sure you're comfortable and focused on one spot and my voice.

When is the last time you remember being sad or angry? Think about what happened to you. What did you do? Can you see the people involved?

Think of how you felt. When did you stop feeling sad or angry? What did you do to feel better?

Remember the story about Peter. He denied Jesus even when he promised not to. Peter cried because of what he'd done. He prayed for help.

Think of a time you felt sad because of something you did. Can you talk to Jesus about it now? Jesus can hear you. He knows how you feel. He has forgiven you. Jesus loves you even when you blow it.

Can you see Jesus looking at you? He's smiling. He's your friend. Talk to him. (Pause for a minute or so.)

5. *The moody questionnaire*—(You'll need a "Moody Questionnaire" handout and a pencil for each person.) Give each person a "Moody Questionnaire" handout and a pencil. Have kids each respond to the four situations.

After everyone has filled out a questionnaire, discuss the answers. Explain that the most helpful responses are: 1—C, 2—B, 3—B, 4—C. These responses let friends share their feelings without thinking they're being judged or put down. Help kids understand that the "right advice" won't do their friends any good until those friends feel they're accepted.

Say: **Some ways to reach out to friends who're down are to:**

(1) encourage them to find something positive in what's happened;

(2) remind them of a good quality or talent they have;

(3) spend a day with them doing something they really like to do;

Moody Questionnaire

Instructions: For each situation, check the quote that best represents how you'd respond.

1. You're going home from school and you see your best friend. You say: "Hi! How's it going?" Your friend says, "This has been the absolute worst day of my life!" You say:

_____(A) "That's no way to be. If you were a Christian you wouldn't have bad days."

_____(B) "Well, with a face like yours who wouldn't have trouble?"

_____(C) "I'm sorry to hear that. Do you want to tell me about it?"

_____(D) "I know what you're talking about—this school is terrible."

2. Your friend has been trying extra-hard to make the basketball team. You say, "I heard today was the final cut; did you make the team?" Your friend says: "No, but the coach had it in for me. He never really gave me a chance." You say:

_____(A) "I know you're upset, but you can't blame the coach."

_____(B) "You must really feel rejected. You really worked hard. What did the coach do that seemed unfair to you?"

_____(C) "There are lots of other things that are more important than basketball."

_____(D) "I know how you feel. That coach is a real jerk."

3. Your friend has just been grounded. You call him or her up and your friend says: "Look, I can't talk. My parents have restricted me for a week because of my grades—I can't even talk on the phone." You say:

_____(A) "Well, how bad were your grades? They can't be as bad as mine."

_____(B) "You think your parents are being too harsh?"

_____(C) "Well, you really should study harder. School is important."

_____(D) "Oh, don't worry! They'll probably forget the restriction in a couple of days."

4. Your friend says: "I'm not going to church tonight; I don't feel like doing anything. So do me a favor and go without me." You say:

_____(A) "Fine, suit yourself."

_____(B) "Come on, this could cheer you up."

_____(C) "Boy, you sound like you feel out of it. What's wrong?"

_____(D) "What could be more important than church? You should keep close to God."

(4) send them a card or note to let them know you appreciate them and are thinking of them;

(5) offer some practical help, such as studying with them to help bring their grades up; and

(6) listen and say nothing.

6. *Goal-setting*—Move back to the happy room for the final discussion on goal-setting. Point out that while we can't stop our emotions, we can control how we respond to them. Challenge kids to set goals that will help them or their friends overcome depression or bad moods. Then have them each find a partner and tell about their goals.

7. *Closing*—(You'll need Bibles, seven "Closing Cheer" handouts and refreshments.) For a joyous ending to the meeting, have kids form seven groups. (A group can be one person—if your group is smaller then seven, have some kids take more than one part.) Give each group a "Closing Cheer" handout and a Bible. Have kids prepare their cheers, then come together again and turn to Psalm 95:1-7a. Read aloud the Psalm one verse at a time and have each group give its cheer after its corresponding verse.

Or have kids read Psalm 95:1-7a and do the cheers in a "rap" style.

Close with prayer and have refreshments.

Closing Cheer

Group #1 Sing for joy, shout aloud!
God is God and we are proud!

Group #2 Music, songs, thanksgiving!
God is God of the living!

Group #3 Lord and King, is our God!
God is God above all gods!

Group #4 Deepest deep, highest high!
God is God above the sky!

Group #5 Land and sea, mountains tall!
God is God, he made it all!

Group #6 Bow your head, bend your knee!
God is God, pray, let it be!

Group #7 Cares for us, our best Friend!
God is God, just say "Amen"!

23 Understanding AIDS

By Mike Gillespie

AIDS is scary and dangerous. Scientists predict that millions will die before they discover a cure. Junior highers need facts and straight talk about AIDS. They need an opportunity to share opinions and develop a Christian approach to the AIDS problem.

Use this meeting to explore AIDS with junior highers.

OBJECTIVES

Participants will:
- learn basic facts about AIDS;
- share fears and opinions about AIDS;
- look at a biblical perspective of compassion and judgment; and
- develop a Christian viewpoint for relating to AIDS victims.

BEFORE THE MEETING

Read the meeting, collect supplies and photocopy handouts.

Ask a high school girl to record a dramatic reading of the "Letter From Sarah" on cassette tape for activity #4.

Find out the name and address of a teenage or adult AIDS victim in your community for activity #6. Contact a nearby hospital or any local AIDS support organizations.

162

THE MEETING

1. *Pullups*—(You'll need a tape player or record player and fast-paced music.) Tell kids to form a large circle with chairs facing the center. Have the kids sit down and have one kid be "It," and have him or her stand in the middle of the circle.

When the music starts, have It run around inside the circle, grab a kid by the hands and "pull up" that person—who then runs along behind It. As they continue around the circle, the end person "pulls up" a new person who falls in line and so on.

When the music stops, everyone must scramble to find a chair. The person left standing is It. Play several rounds and vary the length of time the music is played.

2. *AIDS opinionnaire*—(You'll need an "AIDS Opinionnaire" handout and a pencil for each kid.) Say: **In this meeting we're going to explore a tough topic: AIDS. I'm sure you've all heard or read about this disease. Some of you have strong opinions. We're going to look at how much you know about AIDS, what your feelings are and how we can view AIDS victims from a Christian perspective.**

Give kids each an "AIDS Opinionnaire" and a pencil. Have kids complete the handout.

When they're finished, discuss answers. Ask:

● **What are some reasons for your answers?**

● **Why do you think we have different opinions in our group?**

● **Which of these statements do you have strong feelings about? Why?**

3. *AIDS Tic-Tac-Toe*—(You'll need an "AIDS Fact Sheet" handout for each kid and several large "X" and "O" cards. You'll also need one copy of the "AIDS Tic-Tac-Toe" sheet.) Form two teams. Give one team a supply of "X" cards and the other team a supply of "O" cards.

Set up nine chairs, three-by-three, to form a tic-tac-toe board. Say: **Let's look at facts about AIDS. I'm going to ask a series of questions. If you're the first to raise your hand and correctly answer the question, you'll get to take an "X" or "O" card and sit in a chair in the tic-tac-toe "board." The first team to get three in a row wins the round.**

Play several rounds, using the questions from "AIDS Tic-Tac-

AIDS Opinionnaire

Instructions: Read each statement below. If you feel a statement is true, circle "T." If you feel a statement is false, circle "F."

1. Children and teenagers with AIDS should not be allowed to attend public schools.   T   F

2. A lot of people are really scared about AIDS.   T   F

3. It's just too dangerous to be around someone with AIDS.   T   F

4. People who have AIDS should all be kept together in a safe place away from everyone else.   T   F

5. God is using AIDS to punish sexually sinful people.   T   F

6. The whole world should be concerned about AIDS—not just the United States.   T   F

7. People from other countries who have AIDS should not be allowed to come into our country.   T   F

8. We should spend a lot more money on AIDS research.   T   F

9. Christians should show more compassion for AIDS victims.   T   F

10. I need more facts about AIDS.   T   F

11. I know enough about AIDS to be sure I'll never get it.   T   F

12. I sometimes wonder why God lets a horrible disease like AIDS get started.   T   F

13. I'm afraid to be in the same classroom with someone who has AIDS.   T   F

14. People with AIDS shouldn't be allowed to go to my church.   T   F

15. If I caught AIDS, I wouldn't tell anyone—not even my parents.   T   F

16. It makes me mad to see people doing mean things to AIDS victims.   T   F

17. The names of those who have AIDS should be public knowledge. I have a right to know.   T   F

18. If one of my friends got AIDS, I wouldn't hang around with him or her anymore.   T   F

19. Science will find a cure for AIDS in the next two years.   T   F

20. We should pray for people with AIDS.   T   F

164

AIDS Fact Sheet

● **What does AIDS mean?** Acquired Immune Deficiency Syndrome. Acquired: The disease is caught, not inherited. Immune Deficiency: The defense system that protects the body breaks down and leaves the body susceptible to disease. Syndrome: The disease includes a number of different symptoms.

● **What causes AIDS?** A virus known as Human T-Lymphotrophic Virus Type III causes AIDS in this country. In Europe a virus known as Lymphadenopathy-Associated Virus causes the disease.

● **What about AIDS symptoms?** Symptoms may develop rapidly or the disease may lie dormant for many years. Some people who develop the AIDS antibody may never show the AIDS disorder at all. AIDS symptoms include prolonged fatigue, flu-like symptoms that don't go away, soft white patches in the mouth that don't scrape off, a prolonged sore throat, diarrhea, a dry cough, shortness of breath, swollen lymph nodes, extreme weight loss and purplish blotches on skin.

● **Can a person be exposed to AIDS by casual contact, or by kissing?** There is no proof anyone has ever gotten AIDS by kissing someone with the disease. You can't catch it by touching objects handled by AIDS victims or being around them.

● **Who is most likely to catch AIDS?** Nearly 70 percent of AIDS victims have been homosexual or bisexual men. Almost 25 percent have been intravenous-drug users.

● **Can a person be exposed to AIDS by being vaccinated?** No. This theory has been disproven.

● **Can a person be tested for AIDS?** Yes. The most common test for AIDS only confirms the presence or absence of the antibodies produced in response to the AIDS virus. If this test is positive, additional testing is necessary to confirm exposure to AIDS.

● **How is a person exposed to the AIDS virus?** There are two primary ways. The first is through intimate sexual relations with a person who has the AIDS virus. The second is by intravenous-drug use. Originally a person could have been exposed by receiving blood contaminated by the AIDS virus. But transfusions are no longer a risk since all blood is highly screened for the AIDS virus.

● **Why have we suddenly heard about the AIDS virus?** The AIDS virus has probably been around for a long time but has never been identified until now. Changing lifestyles and sexual promiscuity have created a breeding ground for this deadly disease.

● **How is AIDS treated?** There is no cure for AIDS yet, though certain drugs sometimes prolong the life of AIDS victims.

● **How can I keep from catching AIDS?** Simply avoid exposure to the virus. Do not have sexual relations outside the model that God has established: one man and one woman joining together in marriage as sexually pure persons.

Additional Sources of AIDS Information

AIDS Action Council
729 Eighth St. SE
Ste. 200
Washington, DC 20003
(202) 547-3101

American Foundation for AIDS
   Research
5900 Wilshire Blvd.
Second Floor, East Satellite
Los Angeles, CA 90036
(213) 857-5900

Centers for Disease Control
Box 6003
Rockville, MD 20850
1-800-342-2437

AIDS Tic-Tac-Toe

Instructions: Use these questions to play AIDS Tic-Tac-Toe with your group.

1. What is AIDS an abbreviation for? (Acquired Immune Deficiency Syndrome.)

2. True or false? AIDS is caused when a dangerous bacteria enters the body. (False.)

3. A milder form of the AIDS illness is called ARC. What does that stand for? (AIDS Related Complex.)

4. True or false? Everyone who gets the AIDS virus will develop symptoms quickly and die within a short period of time. (False.)

5. True or false? The AIDS virus works on the body by destroying vital nerve cells. (False. The virus destroys white blood cells—the body's disease fighters.)

6. True or false? A person can catch AIDS by kissing someone who has the disease. (False.)

7. There are two main groups of high-risk people for catching AIDS. Name one of them. (Homosexual or bisexual men, or intravenous-drug users.)

8. True or false? You can catch AIDS by getting vaccinated for other diseases. (False.)

9. True or false? The test for AIDS is sensitive and confirms you have the disease if it's positive. (False.)

10. True or false? Swimming in a pool with someone who has AIDS will subject you to getting the disease. (False.)

11. Name one of the two main ways you can get AIDS. (Intimate sexual relations with someone who has the disease, or intravenous-drug use.)

12. True or false? The AIDS virus is extremely tough and lasts a long time outside the body. (False.)

13. True or false? There are now special drugs available to cure people who get AIDS. (False.)

14. True or false? AIDS is such a powerful disease there is no way to prevent yourself from catching it. (False.)

15. True or false? Being in a room with someone with AIDS opens you to the risk of getting it. (False.)

Toe." At the end of the game, give each kid a copy of the "AIDS Fact Sheet." Look it over together. Help kids understand it.

4. *Letter from Sarah*—(You'll need a tape player, a previously recorded tape of the "Letter From Sarah," newsprint and a marker.) Have kids sit in one group. Say: **Having AIDS is tough. Think about what you would do if you got AIDS.**

Play the tape.

When the tape is finished, have kids tell their reactions. List them on newsprint.

Ask:

● **Do you think God still loves Sarah? Why or why not?**

● **How do you think we as Christians should respond to people like Sarah?**

● **What would you say to Sarah if she walked into our room right now? What would you do?**

5. *A biblical perspective*—(For each group you'll need one section of the "Bible Study Passages and Questions" handout, a Bible and a pencil. You'll also need newsprint and a marker.) Form up to eight groups (a group can be one person). Give each group one section of the handout, a Bible and a pencil. Have each group look up its Bible reference and answer the questions.

When kids are finished, ask a representative from each group to read his or her group's scripture passage and response.

Say: **I want to share some powerful words of Jesus.**

Read aloud Matthew 25:31-46. Discuss how the passage relates to how we should treat people with AIDS. Write kids' responses on newsprint.

6. *Letters to an AIDS victim*—(You'll need a piece of paper, a pencil, and a stamped envelope for each group member, and the name and address of a local teenage or adult AIDS victim written on newsprint.) Give kids each a piece of paper, a pencil and a stamped envelope. Have kids each compose a caring letter to the AIDS victim whose name you've displayed.

When kids finish, have volunteers each read their letter to the group. Collect the letters to mail them.

7. *Closing*—Have kids form a circle. Have each person share one prayer for people with AIDS.

Letter From Sarah

My name is Sarah. I have AIDS. If I was seated next to you right now you'd probably get up and move away, even leave the room. People always do that to me when they find out.

I look normal, just like you. I don't have any horrible signs of the disease. But the tests were positive so I've been exposed to the AIDS virus. I already know what you're thinking: "Fooling around—that got her in trouble." Well you're wrong. I got this stinking disease from a blood transfusion several years ago when I had my appendix out. A lot of us caught it that way. They just didn't know how to test the blood. At least now they do.

I guess I'm eventually going to die from the disease. Do you know how that feels? Knowing something inside you is going to kill you one day. I hate it! I'm a bomb waiting to go off. Any day I could start showing signs of the disease. Then, they tell me I may never show signs at all. How do you even begin to plan a life when you feel there's no life to plan? Nothing seems to matter. What good is it to set goals or want a family or just to have a normal life? You just can't know how it feels to have this horrible thing inside you.

I'm so scared! Nobody cares about me. Everywhere I go people who know I have the disease run away. My parents moved because people were throwing rocks at our house. People left nasty signs on our front door and sent hate mail. You'd think I was a freak or something. Well, I'm not a freak. Doesn't anyone know how badly I hurt inside? I need someone to care.

You stupid people. You can't catch anything by being around me. Talking to me or going to school with me isn't going to give you AIDS. A hug, a smile, a phone call . . . why can't you just show a little kindness?

Do you have any idea what it's like not having a friend . . . not even one? Maybe I should just go ahead and commit suicide. That's what everyone seems to be telling me I should do anyway. You kill me with your fear and your hatred. You kill me with your isolation and your meanness. It's like you hope I go ahead and just do myself in so you don't have to worry about me anymore.

But you know what hurts most of all? Sometimes I think God doesn't even love me anymore. The way you Christians treat me tells me that. If you're supposed to be God's agents of love and caring and support, then why do you shove me away? Maybe God doesn't love me anymore either. What's the use of going on?

I don't know what to do to get you to care about me. Just a kind letter . . . just a phone call . . . just a pleasant conversation . . . how wonderful that'd be. But the best of all would be to have a friend again. I used to take all those for granted. Not anymore.

Would you be my friend? Would you be my friend?

168

Bible Study Passages and Questions

Leviticus 13:45-46
How did the people of Israel treat people who had leprosy? How are our reactions to AIDS victims the same as theirs were to people with leprosy?

Matthew 7:1-5
What does Jesus say about judgment? How does this apply to the way we judge AIDS victims?

Matthew 8:1-4
How did Jesus treat the person who had leprosy? What do you think the people did when they saw Jesus touch someone with leprosy?

Romans 12:1-2
What is Paul's advice to the Romans? What does it mean to you? How does it apply to AIDS?

Romans 12:16-18
What does Paul say about how we should treat one another? What does this say about how we're to treat people with AIDS?

Romans 14:10-13
What does Paul say about judgment? How does this apply to the way we judge AIDS victims?

1 Corinthians 6:19-20
What does Paul say about how we should treat our bodies? What do you think Paul means? What has that got to do with AIDS?

Colossians 3:12-14
What does Paul say about how we should treat one another?
What does this say about how we're to treat people with AIDS?

24 What's So Important About Grades?

By Linda Snyder

Look around your junior high group the week before kids take their end-of-year tests. Maybe you'll see what I see:

- Julie is terrified. Last grading period she got two D's, and her parents grounded her for a month. She's not expecting much better this time.

- Dave is worried too. He knows he's got to make it into a certain university or his parents will be disappointed in him. They've convinced him that every grade counts, even in junior high. There's no excuse for a B—and he knows it.

Kids today feel unprecedented pressure to achieve at school. Success is painted in shades of black and white—high grades mean you've got it; low grades mean you don't.

Use this meeting to help kids put grades in proper perspective. Help them develop realistic expectations and realize life is more than a high GPA.

170

OBJECTIVES

Participants will:

● see how people grade things according to personal likes and dislikes by participating in a taste test;

● discover positive and negative influences to produce high grades;

● rate the apparent success of certain biblical characters to see how bad grades don't necessarily mean failure in life; and

● write realistic expectations of their grades and their future.

BEFORE THE MEETING

Read the meeting, collect supplies and photocopy handouts.

Purchase a large jar of peanut butter for activities #1 and #6. Divide the peanut butter into five numbered bowls. Mix a small amount of salt in the first bowl, sugar in the second, vinegar in the third and vegetable oil in the fourth. Don't add anything to the fifth bowl.

Write each of the phrases from the "Pass, Fail or Draw Cards" box on a separate 3×5 card for activity #2. And create a Pass, Fail or Draw diploma for the game's winning team members.

Photocopy and cut apart the "Ladder of Success Name Cards" handout for activity #4. Find a stepladder to use as a prop.

For each person, make a graduation cap out of posterboard for activity #5. If possible, buy and attach a tassel to each cap.

THE MEETING

1. *Peanut butter taste test*—(You'll need five small bowls of peanut butter—four with added ingredients—and for each person you'll need a spoon, a pencil and a "Taste Test Score Card" handout.) Set the five bowls of peanut butter on a table and have kids line up. Distribute pencils and spoons. Say: **We've been asked by (name of local supermarket) to conduct a taste test for its marketing department. Taste each of the peanut butters and complete your score card.**

Collect the score cards and have an adult volunteer tally the results for use in activity #3. The peanut butter given the highest grades by kids should receive an A. The one receiving the lowest grades should get an F. Tell kids you'll talk about the ratings later.

2. *Pass, Fail or Draw*—(You'll need a watch, a large news-

Taste Test Score Card

Instructions: As you taste the peanut butters, rate each one according to the following qualities. Mark a number from 1 to 5 in each box, according to the following rating scale:

    1=Yuck! 2=Not very good 3=Okay 4=Pretty good 5=Yum!

    Then total the points for each peanut butter and give it a grade according to the grading scale below.

Grading scale: 18 to 20 points = A
                   14 to 17 points = B
                   10 to 13 points = C
                    7 to 9 points = D
                    4 to 6 points = F

	Peanut taste	Thickness	Smell	Texture	Total points	Grade
Brand #1						
Brand #2						
Brand #3						
Brand #4						
Brand #5						

print drawing pad, markers and the Pass, Fail or Draw cards.) Form teams of three or more. Say: **Grades are a big part of your life. The pressure to get good grades is sometimes overwhelming. Maybe you think you're graded by God the same way you're graded at school. In this meeting, you'll discover some of the influences—both good and bad—that surround grades. And you'll learn how God "grades" his children.**

We're going to play Pass, Fail or Draw, a game that's similar to the Win, Lose or Draw game. One by one, each team will pick a representative and come up to the pad. I'll give the representative a card with a word or phrase— either a good or bad influence on grades—to draw on the pad.

Pass, Fail or Draw Cards

Instructions: Write each of these on separate 3×5 cards.

Quiet studying	Studying with television on
Poor teacher	Great teacher
Staying up too late	Drinking
Taking drugs	Report card
Parents' punishment	Cheating
Absent	

Say: **Each team needs to guess the word or phrase its representative draws on the pad. Each team will have 90 seconds to guess. If a correct answer has not been given after 45 seconds, the person drawing should hand the marker and the card to another team member. That person will have another 45 seconds to draw. If your team guesses correctly in 90 seconds, you'll receive 20 points.**

Tell kids the correct answer if they haven't guessed it when time is up. Give another card to the next team. Team members may not speak when it's not their team's turn. Play as many rounds as time allows. Give each winning team member a Pass, Fail or Draw diploma.

3. ***Taste test follow-up***—(You'll need the tallied results of the peanut butter taste test.) Tell kids the results of the taste test, and tell them which peanut butter samples you added ingredients to and which one you didn't. Ask:

● **Now that you know what was in each sample, are you surprised by the test results? Why or why not?**

● **Did you have a hard time grading the different samples? Why or why not?**

● **Is it okay that people disagreed on which sample was the best? Why or why not?**

● **Everyone had different opinions about the quality of the peanut butters; can everyone be right? Why or why not?**

Read aloud 1 Samuel 16:1-7. Say: **Even though you're graded in school by what you produce, God is more interested in what's inside of you. If you were peanut butter and God were the taste-tester, what would he be looking for?**

4. ***Ladder of success***—(You'll need masking tape, a stepladder, a Bible, the "Ladder of Success Name Cards" handout and copies of the "Ladder of Success Questionnaire" handout.) Say: **Grades are important to you, your teachers, parents, employers and college entrance officials. The goal is to do the best you can. But what happens when you get a bad grade? Do you feel bad about yourself? Good grades don't guarantee success. And bad grades don't guarantee failure.**

Place a stepladder in the center of the room. Tell kids it's the Ladder of Success. Explain that each rung represents a grade—A is the top rung and F is the floor. Give six volunteers the six "Ladder of Success Name Cards" from Set A. Have the volunteers read aloud each card and corresponding scripture, one at a time. After each scripture is read, ask kids to grade that Bible character. The grade chosen must be the unanimous choice of the kids, so they'll have to discuss it together.

After kids agree on a grade, have them tape the name card on the appropriate rung. Repeat the same procedure using the cards from Set B.

When all the cards have been taped to the ladder, form groups of four or less and give each group a "Ladder of Success Questionnaire" handout to discuss.

174

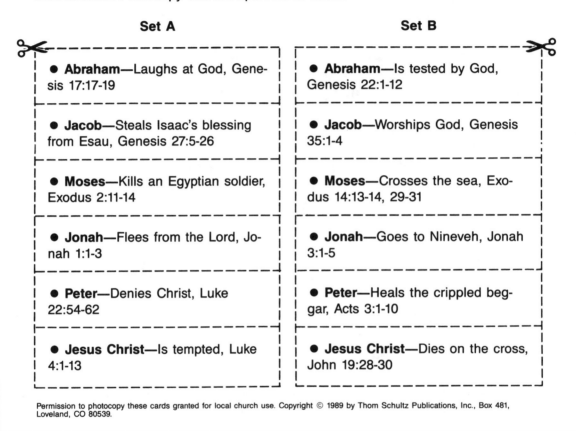

Ladder of Success Name Cards

Instructions: Photocopy and cut apart these cards.

Set A	Set B
● **Abraham**—Laughs at God, Genesis 17:17-19	● **Abraham**—Is tested by God, Genesis 22:1-12
● **Jacob**—Steals Isaac's blessing from Esau, Genesis 27:5-26	● **Jacob**—Worships God, Genesis 35:1-4
● **Moses**—Kills an Egyptian soldier, Exodus 2:11-14	● **Moses**—Crosses the sea, Exodus 14:13-14, 29-31
● **Jonah**—Flees from the Lord, Jonah 1:1-3	● **Jonah**—Goes to Nineveh, Jonah 3:1-5
● **Peter**—Denies Christ, Luke 22:54-62	● **Peter**—Heals the crippled beggar, Acts 3:1-10
● **Jesus Christ**—Is tempted, Luke 4:1-13	● **Jesus Christ**—Dies on the cross, John 19:28-30

5. *Caps off to you*—(You'll need a posterboard graduation cap and a marker for each person.) Tell kids each to divide the top of their cap into four sections and number the sections.

Say: **In section 1, write your grade-point average so far this year. In section 2, write the grade-point average you'd have if you did your very best (it may be the same grade-point average you wrote for section 1). In section 3, write how you feel about the difference or similarity in the grade-point averages you wrote for sections 1 and 2. Then write specific ideas to improve your grades.**

In section 4, write the grade you'd give your life right now—just as you did with Bible characters earlier. Grade your life according to these four categories:

(1) **your relationship with God;**

(2) **your ability to like yourself and work on your faults;**

(3) **your relationships with family members, friends, teachers and other authorities; and**

(4) **how well your actions reflect God's way of doing things.**

Read aloud Romans 8:28, 35-39. Say: **No matter what grade you give yourself, remember that God loves you just as you are. Take your cap home as a reminder of our goal: to grow closer to God.**

6. *Peanut butter worship*—(You'll need five bowls of un-tainted peanut butter and a spoon for each person.) Conduct another taste test using plain peanut butter.

Do you notice a difference in these samples as you compare them with the first set? Why or why not?

Say: **Just like this peanut butter, our "life grades" can improve as we grow closer to God and he removes some of the things that hold us back in life. The Bible characters improved their grades, and so can you. Grades are important, but they are not the beginning and end of the world. Even if you sometimes feel like a failure, God has great plans in store for you.**

Close by having kids each pray for God's help to improve their grade in one specific area.

Ladder of Success Questionnaire

Instructions: Discuss the following questions:

1. How hard was it to give each person a grade? Explain.

2. For the first set of cards, were the grades mostly good or mostly bad? Explain. Did anyone score a high grade? Why or why not?

3. Were the grades higher in the second set of cards? Why or why not? If you had to give an overall grade to each person, what would it be?

4. What's the difference between Jesus' grades and the rest of the grades? Can we be perfect like Jesus is perfect? Why or why not?

5. What's one thing you learned from this activity?

25 *When Stress Weighs You Down*

By Jim Walton

Stress for junior high kids? Adults know what stress is. We're very aware of it. But do junior highers feel stress? Yes. And interestingly enough, many junior highers put pressure on themselves; it's not all from their parents, peers or teachers.

Use this meeting to help kids understand the stresses affecting their lives. Let them experience pressure and then talk openly about their feelings. Help kids learn ways to grow from stress. And show Jesus as the one who gives freedom from the pressures in their lives.

OBJECTIVES

Participants will:
- play a stressful game;
- discover stresses Bible people experienced and how Jesus responded;
- identify and evaluate stresses in their lives;
- discuss ways to support each other during stressful times; and
- celebrate Jesus' promise to give them rest from burdens.

BEFORE THE MEETING

Read the meeting, collect supplies and photocopy handouts.

For activity #3, Cut apart the "Weighty Questions" handout, and attach each section to a different brick or large stone.

For activity #6, gather two stones or two water-filled gallon jugs for each person.

THE MEETING

1. *Stack 'em high*—(You'll need a wide assortment of objects, one for each person. Examples: a tennis racket, a book, a helmet, a magazine, a football, a Frisbee, a pencil, an empty guitar case.) Have everyone stand in a circle and hold one of the objects. On "go," everyone must pass the objects around the circle clockwise. It doesn't matter if a person has more than one object at a time. When you yell "Switch!" everyone must change the direction of the passing to counterclockwise. Keep calling "Switch!" until someone drops something; that person is out. The game continues with the same objects. Before long, only a few kids will be holding and passing many objects. The winner is the last one who hasn't dropped something.

Ask:

● **As the stress increased and you had to hold more objects, how did you feel?**

● **What were you thinking when you had more objects than you had hands to hold them with?**

● **How does this game compare to the stress in your life?**

2. *Agree/disagree*—Have kids sit in a circle. Read aloud the following statements. After each statement, give each group member a chance to simply say "Agree" or "Disagree."

● Teenagers today have more stress than teenagers of previous generations.

● Stress is just anxiety stemming from a person's insecurity.

● My life lacks pressure-free time.

● God uses stress to bring growth.

● Stress is fear.

● Relying on God can reduce stress.

● Relying on God can eliminate stress.

3. *Weighing the scriptures*—(You'll need the five sets of questions from "Weighty Questions"—photocopied and cut apart—each attached to a brick or rock or some other weight, and at least five Bibles.) Form five groups. Give each group a

178

Weighty Questions

Instructions: Cut apart these sections and attach them each to a weight.

✂ --

1. Read aloud Matthew 26:36-46. Discuss:
   ● What weight was Jesus carrying?
   ● If you were Jesus, what would you have prayed for? Why?
   ● If you were one of the disciples, what would you have prayed for? Why?
   ● When you face a tough time, what do you pray for? Why?

2. Read aloud Mark 4:35-41. Discuss:
   ● What weights were the disciples carrying?
   ● What was Jesus' response?
   ● Would you rather have been one of the disciples on the boat—who experienced both fear and calm—or someone on the shore who was watching? Why?
   ● When you're in a stressful situation, what do you pray for? Why?

3. Read aloud Mark 10:46-52. Discuss:
   ● What weight was Bartimaeus carrying?
   ● What kind of person was Bartimaeus?
   ● What was Jesus' response to Bartimaeus?
   ● How did Bartimaeus use the gift Jesus gave him?
   ● How do health concerns weigh you down? What do you pray for?

4. Read aloud Luke 19:1-10. Discuss:
   ● What weight do you think Zacchaeus was carrying as a tax collector?
   ● What was Jesus' response to Zacchaeus?
   ● Why did Zacchaeus say what he did?
   ● How do money-related issues weigh you down? What do you pray for?

5. Read aloud John 3:1-17. Discuss:
   ● What weight was Nicodemus carrying? What was he seeking?
   ● What was Jesus' response to Nicodemus?
   ● What do you think Nicodemus did after talking with Jesus? Why? What would you have done? Why?
   ● What are some things you have questions about and don't understand? What do you pray for?

weight with questions and at least one Bible. Tell each group to read its Bible passage and discuss the questions.

Bring the groups together to share what they discovered.

4. *Stress test*—(You'll need a "Stress Test" and a pencil for each person.) Ask someone to read aloud Psalm 62:1-8. Distribute the "Stress Test" handouts and pencils. Have kids do the tests.

Form groups of four to six to discuss answers.

5. *Discussion*—(You'll need newsprint, a marker and a Bible.) Have everyone sit in a circle. On newsprint, list kids' answers to these questions:

● **What are some stresses you face?**

● **Do these stresses cause or prevent growth? Why?** (Draw stars next to stresses that cause growth; draw circles around stresses that prevent growth.)

● **How can you better handle the stresses that are circled?**

● **How can some stresses that are circled be changed to cause growth instead of prevent growth?**

Encourage kids to think of ways to support each other during stressful times. For example: pray for each other, call a friend and ask how he or she is doing, help with homework, listen. Read aloud Galatians 6:2.

6. *Anchors aweigh*—(You'll need two weights for each person—such as bricks or water-filled gallon jugs, and a Bible.) Have kids line up one in front of the other. Give kids each two weights to hold, one in each hand, straight out from their body. Have a sponsor or young person slowly read aloud Matthew 11:28-30. During the reading, walk down the line of kids and take away their weights; first from one side, then the other.

When the reading is done and the weights are removed, have everyone say "Amen!" As everyone says "Amen!" motion for kids to hold their hands high as a symbol of freedom and thanksgiving.

180

Stress Test

Instructions: For each statement, circle the response(s) that best represents your answer.

1. When things get tough for me, I feel like:

  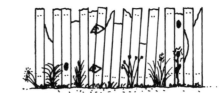

2. Stress makes me:
   (a) love God more.
   (b) doubt God.
   (c) pull away from God.
   (d) angry at God.
   (e) feel nothing different toward God.

3. When I feel a weight burdening me, I:
   (a) seek rest in God.
   (b) find rest in God.
   (c) pray.
   (d) try to carry the load myself.
   (e) don't do anything about it until it crushes me.

Section Six:

VALUES AND DECISIONS

26 Cheating

By Jeanne Leland

Kids cheat in school. Fifty-nine percent of
American teenagers polled in a Gallup Youth
Survey admit to cheating. Fifty-five percent of those
kids also say they regularly attend church. Use this
meeting to help junior highers understand the negative effects of cheating and hear God's challenge to
use their talents to the best of their abilities.

OBJECTIVES

Participants will:
- play a game in which cheating occurs;
- discuss the effects of cheating;
- analyze and role play preventive measures to cheating;
and
- hear God's message of love and challenge to them as
students.

BEFORE THE MEETING

Read the meeting, collect supplies and photocopy handouts.

For activity #1, tape two sheets of newsprint on the wall
about 10 feet apart, each with "Old Testament," "Other" and
"New Testament" written on it. Also, bring fresh cherries with
pits—enough for half the group to have some.

Meet with one group member and ask him or her to cheat
in the "Name the Testament" game (activity #1). Give your pre-
planned cheater a copy of the "Name the Testament" sheet. Tell
this person to arrive early to the meeting, act suspicious and,
when you pretend to search for your "lost" list, to try to get two

cohorts from the team to also look at the answers. Also, explain the purpose of the game and ask your pre-planned cheater to complain about the cherry pits and confess cheating at the appropriate time.

For activity #4, cut two large "C's" and two large "D's" out of red construction paper (one letter per 8½ × 11 page).

For the closing celebration, prepare enough cherry pies and cherry punch for everyone.

THE MEETING

1. *Name the Testament*—(You'll need the two sheets of newsprint you labeled and taped on the wall and a marker. For the winning team, you'll need fresh cherries—enough for everyone on the team.) Have kids form two teams. Have each team choose a newsprint on the wall and line up, one behind the other, facing it. The first person in line should be about 10 feet away from the newsprint.

Tell the group members you'll yell out a name—from the Bible or someplace else. The person at the front of the line for each team should run up to that team's newsprint and use his or her hands to frame the correct source (Old Testament, Other or New Testament). The team that correctly answers the question first gets a point. Say you'll record the teams' points on the sheets of newsprint.

Name the Testament

Old Testament	Other	New Testament
Genesis	Macbeth	Matthew
Exodus	Galactica	Mark
Numbers	Buick	Luke
Judges	Jurors	Acts
Ruth	Poseidon	Romans
Esther	Theseus	2 Corinthians
Psalms	Geometry	Galatians

184

Proceed with the game. Use the books in any order; cross them off once you've called them.

During the game, your pre-planned cheater should arouse suspicion. He or she should sneak peeks at the "Name the Testament" sheet in view of the other team. You should remain oblivious to the cheating. And make sure the team with the cheater wins—even if it means changing the rules midstream; for example, giving three points for each correct answer.

After the game, congratulate the winning team. Award the cherries to the winning kids. The pre-planned cheater should complain about the difficulty of eating the cherries because of the pits. Hopefully, the kids from the other team will accuse him or her of cheating. At this time, react to the comments about the cheating. Ask the kids from the winning team to be honest. Begrudgingly, the pre-planned cheater should admit to cheating. Hopefully, the cohorts will also confess.

Accept the confessions with disappointment. Say: **Cheating takes the glory out of winning for both the cheater and his or her team. Cheating is really the pits!**

2. *Feelings, facts, reasons*—(You'll need newsprint and a marker.) Have everyone sit in a circle.

Tape a sheet of newsprint on the wall and label it "Feelings." Ask group members the following questions. Record their responses on the newsprint.

- **What do you feel like when you cheat?**
- **How do you feel when you get caught cheating?**
- **How does it feel to be part of a winning team—and then find out some of your team members cheated?**
- **How does it feel to lose to cheaters?**
- **How do you think God feels when people cheat?**

Now tape two more sheets of newsprint on the wall. Label one "Facts," and the other "Reasons." Ask kids these questions and record their responses on the appropriate newsprints.

- **What happens to a team when it wins by cheating? Why?**
- **What happens to a professional athletic team when members of the team abuse their talents? Why?**
- **What happens when famous people or politicians misuse other people's trust in them? Why?**
- **Why do kids cheat in school?**
- **What happens when students cheat on homework and tests? Why?**

3. *Cheat sheets*—(For each person, you'll need a "Cheat Sheet" handout and a pencil.) Tell kids there are things they can do so they won't be tempted to cheat. Have kids get with a partner. Give each person a pencil and a "Cheat Sheet" handout. Have kids read the 10 preventive, positive study skills. Have partners think of and write two ways each skill could help them be better students.

Cheat Sheet

Instructions: With your partner, think of and write two ways each skill could help a person be a better student.

I. Attending school regularly
   A.
   B.
II. Taking notes from lectures and from the board
   A.
   B.
III. Taking notes from the textbook
   A.
   B.
IV. Highlighting important facts from the notes
   A.
   B.
V. Reviewing notes regularly
   A.
   B.

VI. Completing and saving all assignments
   A.
   B.
VII. Creating a quiet study area at home
   A.
   B.
VIII. Scheduling study and play time
   A.
   B.
IX. Maintaining good eating and sleeping habits
   A.
   B.
X. Keeping a positive frame of mind
   A.
   B.

---

4. *Deleting cheating*—(You'll need one copy of each of the "Deleting-Cheating Situation Cards." For each "cheater-deleter" group, you'll need a red "C" and "D" and two safety pins.) Form four groups. Designate two groups as cheaters and two as cheater-deleters. Give the groups their "Deleting-Cheating Situation Cards" and give them time to prepare the two skits. Give the two cheater-deleter groups each a red "C" and "D" and two safety pins. Tell them to pin the letters on their cheater-deleter representatives before they enter the skits.

When groups are ready, begin. Preface each skit by announcing the situation.

Discuss skits when finished.

5. *Bible words*—(You'll need the "Cheat Sheets" kids filled out earlier.) Have everyone sit in a circle. Read aloud Ephesians 6:4-5, 9. Have kids interpret God's message of love and challenge for them as students. Say that God's blessed each of them with unique talents. Encourage them to use these to the best of their ability.

Have kids each get their cheat sheets and find a partner. Tell each person to look at the cheat sheet and choose one skill to improve during this school year. Have partners tell each other how the skills they've chosen could help them be better students. Ask them to support each other throughout the year as they work to improve these skills.

6. *Celebration*—(You'll need enough cherry pie and cherry punch for everyone.) Celebrate kids' gifts and abilities by snacking on cherry pie and drinking cherry punch.

Deleting-Cheating Situation Cards

Instructions: Cut apart each skit and distribute them to the appropriate groups.

Cheaters—Skit #1

Situation: The teacher is in the hall talking with another teacher. A major assignment is due. Not everyone finished. Some students are cheating. The teacher walks in on this scene. What does the teacher say and do? What do the cheaters say and do? What are the reactions of the students who weren't cheating?

Characters:
- the teacher
- Tom: His assignment is finished, but he's letting Becky and Sara copy.
- Becky: Her assignment is almost finished, and she's finishing by copying Tom's paper.
- Sara: She forgot to do the assignment altogether. She's copying Tom's paper.
- other students who are not cheating

Freeze Action: Characters maintain positions and expressions without moving when the cheater-deleters arrive.

Cheater-Deleters—Skit #1

Situation: Students have been caught copying answers on a homework assignment. You represent their consciences.

Preparation: Discuss what they should have done so they wouldn't be in this predicament. Select various skills from your "Cheat Sheet" to discuss during the skit. Choose one person to practice speaking in a non-judgmental but know-it-all tone of voice. Pin the red "C" and "D" on that person, who'll be your cheater-deleter representative.

Freeze Action: Watch the scene. When the emotions reach a high intensity, yell together "Freeze." Then send your cheater-deleter to calmly walk in front of the cheaters and say: "Can we talk? Here we have a classic case of some students who didn't follow some simple study skills. What they should have done was . . ."

Cheaters—Skit #2

Situation: You're taking a social studies test. The teacher walks around the room looking for cheaters. The teacher picks up and throws away the tests of the cheating students, who react as indicated.

Characters:
- the teacher
- Dave: He has written notes on the bottom of his shoe. When the teacher catches him, he's ashamed.
- Sally: She has little notes in her pockets. She's outraged when the teacher catches her.
- Linda: She has a case of roving eyes. She's embarrassed when the teacher catches her.
- Bob and Allen: They're whispering answers. When the teacher catches them, they deny everything.
- other students who aren't cheating

Freeze Action: Characters maintain positions and expressions without moving when the cheater-deleters arrive.

Cheater-Deleters—Skit #2

Situation: Students have been caught cheating on a social studies test. You represent their consciences.

Preparation: Discuss what they should have done so they wouldn't be in this predicament. Select various skills from your "Cheat Sheet" to discuss during the skit. Choose one person to practice speaking in a non-judgmental but know-it-all tone of voice. Pin the red "C" and "D" on that person, who'll be your cheater-deleter representative.

Freeze Action: Watch the scene. When the emotions reach a high intensity (after five students are caught), yell together "Freeze." Then, send your cheater-deleter to calmly walk in front of the cheaters and say: "Can we talk? Here we have a classic case of some students who didn't follow some simple study skills. What they should have done was . . ."

Special Series:

By Katie Abercrombie

Drugs, Alcohol and Junior Highers

Drugs and alcohol are serious problems among junior high kids. More than half of ninth-graders claim to be drinkers (they usually take their first drink around age 12), and 7 percent of ninth-graders say they frequently use marijuana, according to a Search Institute survey. And other research reports similar findings.

Use this special three-meeting series to give your group members the opportunity to discuss the facts, their opinions and ways to deal with the problem.

HOW TO USE THIS SERIES

1. Ask your junior highers what would be helpful to them as a part of this series.

2. Talk to your group members about drug and alcohol use in their schools and neighborhoods. Encourage them to bring friends they think need to learn about drugs and alcohol.

3. Decide how much to cover and what you want to emphasize. Adapt these meetings to fit your needs.

4. Read as much as you can on drug and alcohol abuse among young people.

5. Request information from area agencies to use as handouts or as part of your first session.

6. Think about expanding the series by inviting speakers from area agencies or adding films.

Remember that your junior highers—who are at different maturity levels—will be at different levels in their drug and alcohol use and awareness. You may have some kids who are heavily into substance abuse, some who are experimenting and others who have little or no contact with drugs and alcohol.

Again, adapt this series to fit your group. Address all the levels your kids are at. Know where to get help if one of your kids is heavily involved with drugs and alcohol.

27 Exploring the Facts

(Meeting #1)

*T*he average age young people start drinking is 12. Children experiment with drugs around fifth- or sixth-grade. Kids see their peers using drugs and alcohol, and often feel pressure to do the same. Consequently, many junior highers develop serious drug and alcohol problems.

Use this meeting to share information about drugs and alcohol with junior highers and give them the opportunity to discuss concerns they have.

OBJECTIVES

Participants will:
- develop an awareness of drugs and alcohol as a problem among junior highers;
- receive and discuss information about drugs and alcohol, their effects and to what extent junior highers are using them;
- discuss their concerns about drugs and alcohol; and
- celebrate themselves and each other as stars.

BEFORE THE MEETING

Read the meeting and "How to Use This Series" (page 188). Also read the entire three-part series before doing this first meeting. Collect supplies and photocopy handouts.

Find out as much as you can about how serious the drug and alcohol abuse is in your community.

190

THE MEETING

1. ***Make shining symbols***—(You'll need several pairs of scissors. For each person you'll need a piece of construction paper and a marker. Distribute construction paper so that an even number of kids has each color.) Explain to group members that this meeting is about drugs and alcohol, but it's also about them—who they are and what concerns they have about drug and alcohol abuse. Give each person a piece of construction paper and a marker. Make scissors available. Have group members each create a symbol that represents a good feeling they have about themselves. Encourage them to use symbols that shine, such as a candle, a star or a diamond. Have them each include their name on their symbol. Have them leave room to write on their symbol.

After everyone has made a symbol, have kids complete the following sentences on their symbols:

- Something I like about myself is . . .
- Something my friends like about me is . . .
- Something my parents like about me is . . .
- A concern I have about drugs and alcohol is . . .

When everyone's finished, have each person find a partner who has the same-color symbol. Have kids tell their partners what their symbol means, how they completed one of the first three sentences and how they completed the last sentence. Have kids tape their symbols on the wall.

2. ***Fast facts***—(For each person, you'll need a "Fast Facts" quiz and a pencil.) Give each person the "Fast Facts" quiz and a pencil. Have kids mark each statement true or false. Label one side of the room "True" and the other side "False." As you read each question, have junior highers stand by the answer they marked. Then read and discuss the answer to each question.

3. ***Brainstorm concerns***—(For each group of four to six, you'll need a sheet of newsprint and a marker.) Divide the group into groups of four to six, with an adult sponsor in each group. Give a sheet of newsprint and a marker to each group. Have the groups think of things they see happening in their families, schools, neighborhoods and community that result from drug and alcohol abuse. Tell them to list on newsprint ways junior highers are affected by their own or someone else's drug or alcohol abuse. Have each group report to the entire group. Draw

Fast Facts

Instructions: True or false? Place a "T" or "F" to indicate your answer after each statement.

1. Kids in sports or school or church activities and good students are less likely to drink.   T   F

2. The average age young people who drink start drinking is 12.   T   F

3. Most young people don't try drugs until they're in high school.   T   F

4. Over 3 million teenagers nationwide are problem drinkers.   T   F

5. Cigarettes contain no drugs.   T   F

6. Often young people are "turned on" to drugs by older siblings.   T   F

7. The 450 known chemicals in marijuana stay in the body for only several days.   T   F

8. There's no difference between kids drinking and adult social drinking.   T   F

9. Drugs are no longer a problem with teenagers because most of them are experimenting with alcohol.   T   F

10. Young people who have a strong self-esteem, feel good about themselves, and have a strong "support group" tend to resist pressure to use drugs and alcohol.   T   F

Answers to Fast Facts

1. False. All kinds of kids drink.
2. True.
3. False. Often, young people begin experimenting with drugs around fifth- or sixth-grade.
4. True.
5. False. Cigarettes contain two drugs—nicotine and tar.
6. True.
7. False. Chemicals in marijuana stay in the body for a month or more.
8. False. Many kids, by their own admission, drink for the sole purpose of getting drunk.
9. False. Teenagers are trying all kinds of drugs. While use of some types of drugs has declined, use of others—such as cocaine—is increasing.
10. True.

conclusions from what the groups say.

4. *Chemical trivia*—(You'll need the "Chemical Trivia" questions and a stopwatch or a watch with a second hand. For each group of three or four, you'll need a die.) Form teams of three or four. Give each team a die.

Have each team roll its die. The team with the highest number will go first, the team to its left will go second, and so on. The first team begins by rolling its die. The number rolled will be the number of points the team would get for answering its question correctly. The facilitator (who doesn't participate on a team) reads a "Chemical Trivia" question aloud. The team has 10 seconds to discuss before giving its answer. If it doesn't answer correctly, the next team may answer. This can continue through all the teams until a correct answer is given. When a team answers correctly, the facilitator records the score and allows the next team to roll its die.

Play until all the questions have been answered. The amount of time you have will determine how much discussion you allow.

5. *Friendship images*—(For each person, you'll need a piece of paper and a pencil.) Have group members get comfortable, perhaps by lying on the floor or relaxing in chairs. Tell them you're going to have them do some imagining about someone

Chemical Trivia

Instructions: Use these questions in the Chemical Trivia game.

1. True or false? Alcoholism can be influenced by heredity. (True. Genetic influence [heredity] is recognized in 35 to 40 percent of alcoholics.)
2. True or false? Alcohol abuse is physically more damaging more quickly to teenagers than to adults. (True. Because a teenager's body is still growing, alcohol puts an almost unbearable stress on it. Resulting problems include intestinal problems, ulcers in the esophagus, stomach ulcers, liver problems and brain damage.)
3. What are three reasons young people drink? (To relax, cope with stress, be accepted by friends.)
4. What are two common symptoms of teenage drug and alcohol abuse? (Falling grades, problems with family, withdrawn attitude, change in friends, sloppier appearance, weight loss or gain, loss of interest in sports or hobbies.)
5. True or false? Parents are usually suspicious and confront their children when they think they may be drinking or doing drugs. (False. Parents don't want to believe that their kids may be involved in substance abuse.)
6. True or false? Alcohol is safer than other drugs. (False. Like cocaine, heroin, angel dust, and marijuana, alcohol is a mood-altering drug.)
7. What is America's #1 drug problem among young people? (Alcohol.)
8. What is psychological dependency on a drug? (Psychological dependency occurs when a person believes he or she can't do without the drug.)
9. What is physical addiction to a drug? (Without the drug, the body does not feel normal. Stopping the drug causes withdrawal.)
10. Name at least three effects of smoking marijuana. (Increased heart rate; reduced pressure inside eyeball; reddened eyes; bronchitis; sore throat; temporarily reduced coordination; interference with memory; psychological dependency.)
11. What strongly addictive drug is a white powder inhaled or snorted through the nose? (Cocaine.)
12. What is a depressant? (A drug that slows down the nervous system.)
13. Name two depressants. (Alcohol, tranquilizers, sedatives, barbiturates, Quaaludes, Doriden, phenobarbital, Nembutal, Seconal.)
14. What is a stimulant? (A drug that excites the nervous system and increases energy and alertness.)
15. Name two stimulants. (Speed, wake-ups, pep pills, amphetamines, Benzedrine [bennies], Dexedrine, diet pills.)
16. Name at least three dangers of stimulants. (Severe crash after a high; rapid tolerance—more is needed to get high; high blood pressure; irregular heart beat; heart attack; mental illness; severe withdrawal; suicide.)
17. What kind of drugs relieve physical and emotional pain? (Narcotics.)
18. True or false? Most narcotic addicts are street people. (False. A large number of narcotic addicts are from average middle-class families.)
19. Name one mind-altering, or hallucinogenic, drug. (LSD, PCP [angel dust], inhalants [chemicals that are sniffed to get high].)
20. What are two dangers of sniffing chemicals to get high? (Mental confusion or recklessness—can cause accidents; headaches; memory loss; panic; passing out; lung irritation; and liver, heart, kidney, bone marrow or brain damage.)
21. True or false? Pregnant women who smoke are more likely to have a baby born prematurely, underweight or dead. (True.)
22. Which drug causes the most problems in our society? (Alcohol.)
23. What is crack? (A highly addictive, cheap form of cocaine.)
24. What is a person called when he or she can't control the urge to drink? (An alcoholic.)
25. True or false? Young people who abuse alcohol, pot and other drugs often retard the process of growing up and remain immature because they hide their feelings behind drugs. (True.)

they're concerned about.

Say the following, allowing plenty of time between statements for kids to think and imagine: **Think of someone you know who's involved with drugs or alcohol in a harmful way. This could be a friend, a family member, a neighbor, even yourself—just someone you're concerned about, someone you're worried about. If you don't know anyone with a problem like this, choose someone you know you'd be concerned about if he or she had a problem with drugs or alcohol. What is he or she doing? What does he or she look like? How are drugs or alcohol affecting this person in areas of family, school, friends, appearance, physical health? What do you see in the future for this person? How do you feel toward this person? How do you feel about what he or she is doing? What would you like to say to him or her?**

Then have kids get into a circle. Hand out paper and pencils. Have kids each write these things while they're still fresh in their mind:

● a general description of the situation, using no names or anything else that would identify the person;

● effects of this person's drug or alcohol problem;

● how they feel about the situation; and

● what they'd like to say to the person.

Give group members time to write. Then have them find their partners from activity #1 and share what they wrote.

6. *Star affirmations*—(For each person, you'll need a pencil, scissors and several sheets of construction paper.) Say: **A strong self-esteem is important in avoiding the pitfalls of drug and alcohol abuse. People with strong self-esteem like themselves, are comfortable being themselves and can appreciate others for their positive characteristics.**

The Apostle Paul talks about Christians shining "like stars in the universe" (Philippians 2:15). **You can be a shining light in somebody's dark world. Other kids may see you as somebody they want to be like. You don't have to be like everybody else. You can shine brightly.**

Our self-esteem is influenced by what others think of us and what they say to us. In our next activity, we'll give each other's self-esteem a lift.

Distribute pencils, scissors and construction paper. Have kids each cut out a construction paper star for every other person in the room. Have kids each write the name of each person in the group on a separate star along with something they admire about that person. Tell kids to give stars to the people whose names are on them.

7. *Shining prayers*—Close the meeting with a short prayer of thanks for all the shining people in your group. Do a group hug or individual hugs before leaving.

28 Clarifying Values

(Meeting #2)

Junior highers, like most people, have beliefs, goals, friends, activities or possessions they value highly. They may also have beliefs such as "it's wrong to steal," "it's important to help others" or "drinking and driving don't mix."

Involvement with drugs and alcohol can cause a young person to give up something highly valued or act contrary to beliefs.

Use this meeting to help junior highers look at what's important to them and how drugs and alcohol affect their values.

OBJECTIVES

Participants will:
- brainstorm reasons why people abuse alcohol and drugs;
- clarify their values regarding drugs and alcohol;
- evaluate how drugs and alcohol could affect things they value;
- explore what values media, parents, friends and God present about drugs and alcohol; and
- express and hear what they value about one another.

BEFORE THE MEETING

Read the meeting, collect supplies and photocopy handouts.

For activity #3, make four yellow construction paper stars numbered 1, 2, 3 and 4. Place one in each corner of the meeting room.

For each group of four to six in activity #4, gather an assortment of magazine advertisements, written descriptions of scenes from popular movies (or TV shows or books), or popular song lyrics that say something about drugs and/or alcohol.

Also, on a sheet of newsprint, write the questions listed in activity #4.

Photocopy and cut apart the message cards in activity #5.

On another sheet of newsprint, write the incomplete sentences listed in activity #6.

Gather a candle and some matches for activity #7.

THE MEETING

1. *Charades*—Divide the group into teams of four to six to play Charades. Make sure there's an adult sponsor in each team. Have each team pantomime something the team members enjoy doing. Have other teams try to guess the answer.

After the game explain that people often enjoy doing things because of what's important to them. People may also do things that they don't enjoy because of what's important to them. When people become involved with drugs and alcohol, they may give up things that are important to them.

2. *Brainstorming*—(For each group you'll need a sheet of newsprint, a marker and masking tape.) Give each group a sheet of newsprint and a marker. Have them spend three to five minutes thinking of reasons people drink or take drugs and write the reasons on their newsprint. Have each group tape its list on the wall and read it to the entire group. Ask the groups to clarify any reasons people don't understand. (Some examples of reasons people drink or take drugs are to relax, escape, feel more adult, get high or drunk, be accepted, rebel against authority and to look cool.)

3. *Four stars of values*—(You'll need the four yellow construction paper stars, each placed in a different corner of the room. For each person, you'll need a "How Do I Shine?" hand-

198

out and a pencil.) Distribute the "How Do I Shine?" handouts and pencils, and give group members a few moments to complete the handout.

Have kids stand. Point out the four stars in the four corners of the room. Explain that you'll read a situation from the handout and they each should stand near the star whose number represents their response to the situation. Read the first situation. When the participants have chosen their corners, begin with the corner with the fewest people and ask the groups each to explain why they chose that answer. Do this with all of the situations, allowing time for group members to discuss and express their values.

4. *Media messages*—(You'll need a sheet of newsprint with the four discussion questions written on it. For each group, you'll need an assortment of magazine advertisements, descriptions of scenes from popular movies, TV shows or books, and popular song lyrics that say something about drugs and/or alcohol.) Say: **We're all influenced by what we see and hear in the media. Often what we wear, buy or do is something we've heard or seen on television, radio, movies or other forms of media.**

Have group members get back in their groups of four to six. Hand out magazine advertisements, descriptions of scenes from popular movies, TV shows or books, and popular song lyrics that say something about drugs and/or alcohol. Display the newsprint with the following questions. Have group members discuss:

● What does this "media item" tell us about drugs and/or alcohol?

● What kind of people drink in the media and/or take drugs?

● What are the good things the media tell us about drugs and alcohol?

● What are the bad things the media tell us about drugs and alcohol?

After the groups have discussed these questions, have each group share some of its observations with the whole group.

5. *Comparing messages*—(For each group, you'll need a piece of posterboard, pencils, markers and a message card from page 201.) Say: **We're all bombarded with conflicting messages about drugs and alcohol. In one evening of TV viewing, we're likely to see an advertisement for a**

How Do I Shine?

Instructions: Choose how you would respond to each situation.

I know my best friend is using drugs several times a week. I would . . .

1) ignore it.

2) drop him or her.

3) encourage him or her to get help.

4) tell someone in authority.

I found drugs hidden in my house and I suspect they belong to my sister. I would . . .

1) leave them where I found them.

2) flush them down the toilet.

3) confront my sister.

4) tell my parents.

I'm at a party where drugs are readily available. I would . . .

1) go home.

2) stay but don't try any.

3) do what everyone else is doing.

4) just try a little.

I'm at a friend's house with a group of my closest friends. No adult is present. One of my friends pulls out a bottle of liquor and starts passing it around. I would . . .

1) take a sip.

2) skip it, but pass it on.

3) leave.

4) encourage my friends not to drink.

A guy (or girl) who I'm really interested in invites me to go to a party with him (or her) and emphasizes that there'll be plenty of "liquid refreshment." I don't want to drink, but I really want to be with this person. I would . . .

1) make up an excuse not to go.

2) go but don't drink.

3) say I can't go but invite him or her over to my house to watch a video next weekend.

4) go to the party so he or she won't think I'm a little kid.

200

painkiller, another for cold medicine, yet another for beer, and then an anti-drug promotion. The Bible condemns drunkenness (Ephesians 5:18) but Jesus may have thought drinking was appropriate on certain occasions (John 2:1-10 and Luke 22:17-18). Obviously, there must be a difference between responsible and irresponsible use of drugs and alcohol.

Form eight groups (four if you have fewer than 16 kids). Give each group a piece of posterboard, pencils, markers and a message card. If you have only four groups, give each group two message cards and two pieces of posterboard.

Explain that each group is to make a poster encouraging responsible use or discouraging irresponsible use of drugs and alcohol. Each group's message card will explain what to do. Encourage the groups to be specific in their choice of situations.

When the groups have finished the posters, have each group explain its advertisement. Put the posters on the wall.

An alternative to this activity is to use the same message cards to develop and present television or radio commercials.

6. *Putting it all together*—(You'll need the sheet of newsprint with open-ended statements listed on it.) Have group members sit in a circle on the floor. Display the newsprint with the following incomplete sentences. Have kids each choose one to complete and share with the group.

● Something I learned today that I hadn't thought of before is . . .

● Something I learned about myself today is . . .

● Something I still have a question about is . . .

● Something I plan to do differently because of this meeting is . . .

7. *Valuing one another*—(You'll need a candle and matches.) Have kids each think about the person on their left. Ask:

● **What is something you value about that person?**
● **How does that person shine for you?**

Light the candle. Say a short prayer of thanks for what's special and valuable to you about the person on your left. Then pass the candle to that person. He or she should do the same for the person on his or her left. When everyone has said a prayer, close the meeting by thanking God for all of the valuable people in the room who shine so brightly for each other.

Message Cards

Message Card #1—Look for messages (in newspapers, magazines, books, movies, television, music) that promote responsible or healthy use of drugs and alcohol. Make an advertisement to express it. (Example: If you drink, don't drive; if you drive, don't drink.)

Message Card #2—Look for messages in media that promote irresponsible or unhealthy use of drugs or alcohol. Make an advertisement to discourage it. (Example: If the media example is a soap opera star abusing tranquilizers, the poster might feature an ad that encourages people to use drugs only on the advice of a physician.)

Message Card #3—What positive messages do your parents give you about drugs and alcohol? Do they say it's okay to have a glass of champagne on special occasions? Do they use or encourage you to use over-the-counter drugs responsibly? Do they avoid drinking and driving? Choose a situation and make an advertisement to express it. (Example: Pain killers can be killers.)

Message Card #4—What negative messages do your parents give you about drugs and alcohol? Is drinking wrong in all situations or just in certain ones? What drugs or drug-related situations do they caution you to avoid? Choose a situation and make an advertisement to express it. (Example: You can crack up over Crack.)

Message Card #5—In what ways do your friends encourage you to use drugs and alcohol responsibly? How do they encourage you to remain drug- and alcohol-free? Choose a situation and make an advertisement to express it. (Example: Friends don't let friends drink and drive.)

Message Card #6—In what ways do your friends encourage you to use drugs or alcohol irresponsibly? What kinds of pressure do you feel from friends to use drugs or alcohol in a way that would be against your values? Choose a situation and make an advertisement that discourages the reader from using drugs irresponsibly. (Example: Everybody is not doing it.)

Message Card #7—Think about some positive messages in the Bible about drinking. Look at Psalm 104:14-15 and John 2:3. Make an advertisement that expresses what God says about drinking responsibly. (Example: Know your limits.)

Message Card #8—Think about some negative messages in the Bible about drinking. Look at Proverbs 20:1; Proverbs 23:20-21; and Romans 13:13. Make an advertisement that expresses what God says about drinking irresponsibly. (Example: One drink too many can ruin your whole life.)

29 Facing Peer Pressure

(Meeting #3)

*J*unior highers are particularly susceptible to peer pressure because they need to be accepted and belong. They may do certain things—such as drink or take drugs—not because they want to, but because they're afraid to go against the crowd. They fear they won't be included in the group and will lose important relationships.

Use this meeting to help junior highers look for positive ways to deal with drug-related peer pressure.

OBJECTIVES

Participants will:
● experience pressure to conform to the group;
● discuss what peer pressure is, how it feels and what things people feel pressured to do;
● look at how peer pressure relates to them;
● explore what God has to say about conforming and about alternatives to drinking; and
● act out positive ways to respond to negative peer pressure.

BEFORE THE MEETING

Read the meeting, collect supplies and photocopy handouts. For activity #1, bring enough candy for kids each to have a piece. For every group of eight you'll need seven instruction cards that say, "Don't eat your candy until everyone else does," and one card that says, "Don't eat your candy under any circumstances."

Have someone prepare punch and cookies for refreshments.

THE MEETING

1. *Sweet greetings*—(For each person, you'll need a piece of candy and an instruction card.) Form groups of no more than eight kids. Have group members sit in a circle. Give each group member a piece of candy and an instruction card. Give all but one of the members of each group the instruction, "Don't eat your candy until everyone else does." Give the remaining member of each group the instruction, "Don't eat your candy under any circumstances." Tell kids not to show their instructions to anyone else. Allow several minutes.

Then get everyone together and ask:
* **How did you feel while waiting to eat your candy?**
* **Did you eat your candy? Why or why not?**
* **Did someone not eat the candy?**
* **How did you feel about that person?**
* **What did you say or do to that person?**

Specifically ask the kids who didn't eat the candy:
* **How did it feel not to do what everyone else was doing?**
* **How did you respond?**
* **What did you do when (if) the rest of the group pressured you to eat your candy?**

If the person who wasn't supposed to eat the candy ate it, discuss why.

2. *What is peer pressure?*—(You'll need newsprint and a marker.) Gather everyone in a circle. Explain that this session deals with drug- and alcohol-related peer pressure. Have group members define peer pressure. List definitions on newsprint. Include that peer pressure is pressure from friends, schoolmates, neighbors or family to do something that someone might not do without the pressure. Emphasize that peer pressure can encourage someone to do things that are good or bad.

3. *Pressure points*—(You'll need newsprint and a marker.) Have each person think of several things people do because of peer pressure. Have each person give one reason why people give in to peer pressure. Write the reasons on newsprint.

4. *What's your pressure rating?*—(For each person, you'll need a "What's Your Pressure Rating?" handout and a pencil.) Distribute the "What's Your Pressure Rating?" handouts. Read the directions with the group and give everyone a few minutes to answer the questions.

Discuss the results with the group and draw conclusions about whose pressure the group members are most likely to respond to. Ask:

● **What kinds of things do young people do because of peer pressure?**

● **How is pressure from friends different from pressure from parents or God?**

● **What could happen if someone didn't give in to peer pressure in some of these areas? How could that affect the person?**

Emphasize that one of the main reasons people yield to peer pressure is because they want to be accepted by other people.

5. *What does God say?*—(For each group of four, you'll need a Bible and a "Star Scripture Card.") Form groups of four. Give each group a Bible and a "Star Scripture Card." It's okay for more than one group to have the same card. Tell each group to follow the instructions on its card, and have each group choose a volunteer to represent their group.

Give the groups a few minutes to read and discuss their passages. Have volunteers share with the whole group by reading their passages and summarizing their discussion and conclusions about maintaining good friendships while resisting negative peer pressure.

6. *Acting out star situations*—(You'll need a copy of the "Star Situations" sheet, cut apart and placed in a basket or hat.) Form six groups (a group may be as small as two people). Have each group draw one of the "Star Situations" from the basket (or hat). Have each group read its situation and think of ways to respond without insulting or losing friends. Each group should choose its favorite response and make up a short drama of the situation and response. After each group performs its drama, applaud. Then ask the rest of the group members to think of other effective responses.

What's Your Pressure Rating?

Instructions: Below are some situations in which people often feel pressure to behave a certain way. Read each situation and think about what you would do. Decide whose pressure you'd respond to and check the appropriate boxes. Not all responses fit all the situations. You may have more than one check for some situations and no checks for other situations.

	I	my best friend	a group of friends	my parents	God	
1. I would wear my hair a certain way because						expected me to.
2. I would buy a certain brand of clothing because						expected me to.
3. I would go to a party with someone I didn't really like because						expected me to.
4. I would drink one beer when everyone else was drinking because						expected me to.
5. I would smoke marijuana with a group of people because						expected me to.
6. I would leave a party if people were using drugs because						expected me to.
7. I would ignore someone who wanted to be my friend because						expected me to.
8. I would shoplift a piece of jewelry from a store because						expected me to.
9. I would smoke a cigarette because						expected me to.
10. I would say no to a drink because						expected me to.
11. I would go to a church retreat because						expected me to.

206

Star Scripture Cards

✂ -

Star Scripture Card #1   Read Romans 12:2.
   Discuss what you think this means in terms of how you respond to peer pressure. Think of ways you can respond to God's will and have good relationships with your friends.

Star Scripture Card #2   Read Ephesians 5:18.
   Discuss what you think it means to be filled with the Spirit. How does a person who's filled with the Spirit treat his or her friends? Think of ways a person who chooses to be filled with God's Spirit—rather than respond to pressure to drink or try drugs—can have good peer relationships.

Star Scripture Card #3   Read Daniel 3:16-18.
   Discuss what you think these three young men were feeling when they addressed the king. Think of ways you can say no to peer pressure and still maintain good relationships with your friends.

Star Scripture Card #4   Read Daniel 6:10-13.
   Discuss what you think Daniel felt when he disobeyed the king's command. Think of ways you can be different and still keep friends.

Star Situations

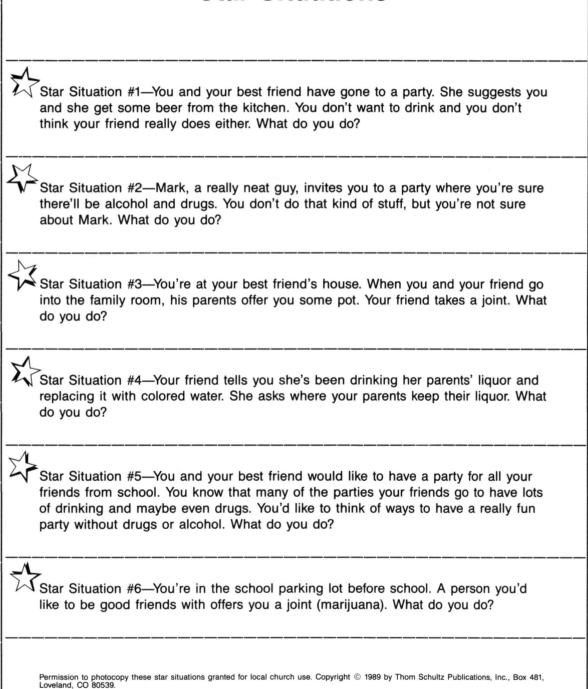

Star Situation #1—You and your best friend have gone to a party. She suggests you and she get some beer from the kitchen. You don't want to drink and you don't think your friend really does either. What do you do?

Star Situation #2—Mark, a really neat guy, invites you to a party where you're sure there'll be alcohol and drugs. You don't do that kind of stuff, but you're not sure about Mark. What do you do?

Star Situation #3—You're at your best friend's house. When you and your friend go into the family room, his parents offer you some pot. Your friend takes a joint. What do you do?

Star Situation #4—Your friend tells you she's been drinking her parents' liquor and replacing it with colored water. She asks where your parents keep their liquor. What do you do?

Star Situation #5—You and your best friend would like to have a party for all your friends from school. You know that many of the parties your friends go to have lots of drinking and maybe even drugs. You'd like to think of ways to have a really fun party without drugs or alcohol. What do you do?

Star Situation #6—You're in the school parking lot before school. A person you'd like to be good friends with offers you a joint (marijuana). What do you do?

208

7. *Celebrating alternatives*—(You'll need a sheet of newsprint with Romans 12:2 written on it.) For a closing worship celebration, give kids each a piece of paper and have them tear it into the shape of a star. Then have them each write on it some things they do for fun that don't involve drugs or alcohol. Read Romans 12:2 aloud to the group. Have group members tape their stars one by one on the newsprint with Romans 12:2 written on it. As each person tapes his or her star on the newsprint, he or she should tell the group one or two positive alternatives to drugs and alcohol. After everyone has had a turn, pray for God's help in finding creative ways to have fun and resist peer pressure to do harmful things. Close with hugs.

8. *Refreshments*—Invite everyone to enjoy punch, cookies and friendship before they go.

30 *Lying*

By Lee Hovel

Research by Search Institute shows that approximately 85 percent of all junior highers lie to their parents. The research also shows that the older junior highers get, the less they think lying is wrong.

Use this meeting to show junior highers how lies are like a bunch of feathers in the wind—once released, they're difficult to gather up again. Discuss consequences of lies with your kids. And guide them through what the Bible says about lying.

OBJECTIVES

Participants will:
- play a game to experience the consequences of telling lies;
- discuss why people lie, and discover that lies hurt relationships;
- experience what scripture says about lying; and
- experience an activity to celebrate "bearing positive witness."

BEFORE THE MEETING

Read the meeting, collect supplies and photocopy handouts.

Write each statement in activity #1 on a separate sheet of newsprint. Tape the newsprint statements on the walls of the room. Also for activity #1, gather nine red round stickers for each person.

For activity #3, fill two quart-size freezer bags with confetti. Become familiar enough with the story in activity #3 so you can tell it without using notes.

Cover a shoe box with white paper and label it "Truth or Consequences Box." Stuff the box with situations from "Truth or Consequences Situations" on page 213. (Photocopy them and cut them apart.)

For every four to six group members, prepare at least one construction paper feather with a Bible reference from activity #5 written on it. Recall a personal story to share in activity #5 concerning your experience with a lie.

For activity #6, prepare enough blank construction paper feathers so your adult workers each can have one for each young person.

For refreshments (activity #7), bring unpopped popcorn and several hot-air popcorn poppers. For each person, bring a Dixie cup.

THE MEETING

1. *Is it okay to lie?*—(You'll need nine sheets of newsprint hung on the wall, each with a different statement from the list below written on it. For each person, you'll need nine red sticker circles.) As kids arrive, give them each nine red sticker circles. Tell kids to walk around and read the statements on the wall. Have them each stick a red circle under any statement they agree with. The statements:

● If I had chopped down the cherry tree, I would have admitted it.

● If I'd been Pinocchio, I would have liked to stay out of trouble.

● It's always wrong to tell a lie.

● A little white lie never hurt anyone.

● A lie is okay if it makes someone feel good.

● If I have kids, I'll tell them there's a Santa Claus and an Easter Bunny.

● I tell three to five lies a day.

● I've been hurt by someone lying to me or about me.

● I've never told a a lie.

Based on the placement of red stickers, discuss the group's feelings about lying.

2. *Lie detectors*—(You'll need a chalkboard and chalk.) Form groups of four to six. Write the following descriptions on a chalkboard:

- The person you most admire
- Your biggest worry, anxiety or fear
- Your most prized possession
- A future profession or job you hope to have

Have kids each respond to these statements, but instruct them each to make one answer a lie. After each person responds, have other group members guess which of the responses is actually the lie. Have the person reveal which response is a lie.

3. *Feathers in the wind*—(You'll need two freezer bags of confetti and the story, "Feathers in the Wind.") Form two equal-size groups. Have two adult sponsors stand on chairs in the middle of the two groups. Tell junior highers to catch as much confetti as possible before it hits the floor. Give the sponsors the bags of confetti and have them throw the confetti high in the air. See which group catches the most confetti.

Then have the groups look at how much confetti is on the floor. Have everyone sit in a circle. Tell the story, "Feathers in the Wind."

Discuss kids' reactions to the story.

Feathers in the Wind

One day a woman went to St. Francis of Assisi and confessed that she was guilty of spreading malicious gossip. She asked him what she could do to be forgiven. St. Francis told her to pluck a goose and lay one feather on the doorstep of each person she'd said malicious things about.

The woman went away hurriedly and did as she was instructed. She returned to St. Francis to ask the next step. He sent her back to gather each feather she placed on the doorsteps. But she discovered that the feathers had blown all over town.

When she returned the second time, St. Francis said: "You may wish to repent, and that is good. But you can never recall the words that you have spoken. They have gone on their way, doing harm. You have committed a sin for which no amends can be made. Confess your sin to God and ask for his forgiveness, for God is the only one who can forgive you."

Reprinted from *The Ten Commandments*, Learner Book, Affirm Series, copyright © 1984 Augsburg Publishing House.

4. *Truth or consequences*—(You'll need four sheets of newsprint and a marker. You'll also need the Truth or Consequences Box.) Briefly describe some reasons people lie. Use these categories:

● Hide—People lie to hide the truth so they don't have to face the consequences.

● Hurt—People gossip and tell lies about others to hurt them.

● Help—People lie because they believe their lies really help other people in some way.

● Honor—People lie to make themselves look better.

Tape on the wall four sheets of newsprint and label them "Hide," "Hurt," "Help," and "Honor."

Have a volunteer take a situation out of the Truth or Consequences Box. Have the volunteer read the situation aloud.

Have group members decide the reason this person might've told the lie. Teach kids these actions to indicate which category they think the lie fits in:

● cover eyes—Hide;

● punch—Hurt;

● hold hand out, palm up—Help; and

● pat themselves on the shoulder—Honor.

After the group agrees which category the lie fits in, have kids each find a partner. Give partners 30 seconds to discuss how the lie could hurt. Then have kids tell some things they discussed. List their responses on the appropriate sheet of newsprint.

Follow the same steps until the group has evaluated every situation in the box.

5. *Lies and God*—(You'll need two sheets of newsprint and a marker. For each group, you'll need one or more construction paper feathers, each with one reference on it from the list below.) Have kids get back into the groups of four to six they were in for activity #2. Give each group at least one construction paper feather, each with a different one of these Bible references on it:

● Exodus 20:16   ● Deuteronomy 5:30

● Proverbs 6:16-19   ● Proverbs 18:6-8

● Zechariah 8:16-17   ● Matthew 26:69-75

● Acts 5:1-11   ● Colossians 3:12-17

● Ephesians 4:15-16, 25-32   ● James 1:26; 3:4-10

Display two large sheets of newsprint. Label one "God's Judgment" and the other "God's Encouragement." Have each

Truth or Consequences Situations

A friend asks if you like what he or she is wearing; you lie and say yes.

You're the new kid at school; you tell all kinds of glamorous stories about yourself (well, they aren't *all* untrue).

You and your friend have a fight; you tell other kids nasty things about your friend.

You're an hour late coming home on a Friday night; you tell your parents an incredible story about a traffic jam, getting lost, and so on.

Your friend asks you to tell his parents he was at your house last night, when in fact he was at a party. When the parents call, you say your friend was with you all night.

You see your best friend cheating on a test; your class operates on the honor code, but you don't turn your friend in.

Your grandfather is terribly ill with cancer, and your parents say not to tell your grandfather he's dying. Your grandfather asks you if he's dying; you say, "I don't know."

You lie and say you really like someone and want to be friends; this person finds out from others that you really can't stand him or her.

group read its passage, and determine whether the passage gives a judgment or encouragement. Have each group explain its answer(s) to the entire group. Write a summary statement for each passage on the appropriate sheet of newsprint.

Summarize what God's Word says about lying. Perhaps share a brief personal story that shows how the scriptures apply. Pray that kids will respond to God's encouragement in their relationships with each other.

6. *A feather in your cap*—(For each person you'll need a pencil, scissors and several sheets of construction paper.) Distribute the construction paper feathers. Have kids each cut out as many construction paper feathers as there are people present (excluding themselves). Have kids each write the name of a different person in the group and something positive about that person on each of the feathers. Make sure adult sponsors each write a positive statement about each group member to be sure no one is left out. Get everyone together. Have everyone throw the feathers into the air. Then have each person pick one up. (If a person gets one with his or her name on it, he or she should put it back.) Quickly have kids each read the name on their feather and the positive statement. Repeat this exercise two or three times. Finally, have kids each find all the feathers with their name on them. Encourage kids to take them home as "feathers in their cap."

7. *Refreshments*—(You'll need unpopped popcorn and several hot-air popcorn poppers. For each person you'll need a Dixie cup.) Place several hot-air popcorn poppers around the room. Get the poppers started and give kids each a Dixie cup to catch the popcorn. Have kids catch their popcorn snack in the air.

31 *Risky Business*

By Kurt Bickel

*L*ife is a risky business.

And junior highers are some of the biggest risk-takers of all. According to a survey by the U.S. Department of Health and Human Services, teenagers make wrong decisions about their health and safety even when they know the destructive consequences of their actions. The results of the survey show "too many young people, even when they know better, don't always make the right health decisions," says Dr. Robert E. Windom, assistant health secretary of the U.S. Public Health Service.

Use this meeting to challenge kids to take a hard look at their risky behavior. Help them step into healthy risks and walk away from destructive ones.

OBJECTIVES

Participants will:
- determine the difference between good and bad risk-taking;
- find out how much they are willing to risk in life;
- evaluate the risks taken by biblical characters; and
- make a practical commitment to avoid bad risks and seek healthy risks.

216

BEFORE THE MEETING

Read the meeting, collect supplies and photocopy handouts.

Collect a large quantity of building blocks from the church nursery, the church children's department, or a child-care center for activity #1.

Find three, 8-foot 2×4 boards and an umbrella for activity #3. (You may substitute masking tape for the boards if necessary.)

THE MEETING

1. *The block tower*—(You'll need building blocks.) Form two or three equal teams. Give each team an equal number of blocks. Say: **Your team's goal is to build the highest tower of blocks possible. Team members will take turns placing blocks, one at a time, on their tower. Blocks must be placed one on top of the other. Each round, one team member can place one block on the team's tower.**

Each block placed successfully on the tower is worth two points. A person can pass on his or her turn and still score two points, but he or she may pass only once (notice the team receives two points on a passed turn, but the tower doesn't grow taller). You should keep track of how many people pass their turn and total the passed-turn points at the end of the game.

The tallest tower is worth an additional 20 points. But if your tower falls, your team loses 30 points (subtracted from the total number of blocks used before the tower fell). Your team can decide together to stop building your tower during your turn. When one tower falls, or when all teams decide to stop building, the game is over. The team with the most points at that time wins.

Play the game. Ask:

● **Did this game reward or punish risk-taking? Explain.**

● **Were some people in your group more willing to take a risk than others? Why or why not?**

● **Did your team members help you decide what to do or did they make you do it? Explain.**

● **In your own life, who most often decides what risks you will take? friends? family? God? you?**

Say: **Every day we take risks—with our bodies, with friends, even with God. Some risks are foolish and dan-**

gerous, others are wise and courageous. The key is to cut down on foolish risks and increase the number of wise risks we take.

2. *Where do you draw the line?*—(For each person you'll need a "Where Do You Draw the Line?" handout and a pencil.) Distribute pencils and have kids each complete a "Where Do You Draw the Line?" handout.

Read aloud Philippians 2:3-9. Ask:
● **If Jesus had completed this handout, what would his Risk Factor have been?**
● **In his life, did Jesus take more risks than you? Explain.**
● **What was different about the risks Jesus took compared with the risks you take?**

3. *Life on a tightrope*—(You'll need three 8-foot 2×4s—or a roll of masking tape—and an umbrella.) Set the 2×4s end to end across your meeting room (or make a long line on the floor with a strip of masking tape). Have a volunteer "walk the tightrope." Give that person an umbrella for balance and have him or her walk down and back on the "tightrope." Have group members who thought the tightrope walk was risky stand up. Then have those who would be willing to ride on the shoulders of the walker stand. Have those who stand climb, in turn, onto the walker's shoulders and do it.

If no one volunteers, ask kids why they refused. If someone does volunteer, ask what motivated him or her.

Then ask:
● **If the 2×4s were nailed and placed across a deep ravine, would you walk the tightrope? Why or why not?**
● **If the 2×4s spanned the roofs of two high rises and provided your only way out of a burning building, would you walk the tightrope?**
● **Would you do it if you felt God wanted you to?**
Read aloud Matthew 16:24-25. Ask:
● **What kind of risk is Jesus talking about?**
● **Does the risk seem too great to you? Why or why not?**

4. *God's risk-takers*—(You'll need the "God's Risk-Takers Cards." For each person you'll need a Bible and a marker.) Say:
Long ago, God was the only ruler the people of Israel

Where Do You Draw the Line?

Instructions: Circle each risk you would be willing to take.
Concerning parents:
    1. Do what my parents ask me to do.
    2. Tell my parents that my grades are good when they're really bad.
    3. Come home two hours later than my parents asked me to.
    4. Tell my parents I'll leave for good if they keep bugging me.

Concerning friends:
    1. Put my friends' needs before my own.
    2. Tell my friends who I'd like for a girlfriend or boyfriend.
    3. Tell a secret about my best friend to someone else.
    4. Steal my best friend's boyfriend or girlfriend if I really liked him or her.

Concerning travel:
    1. Ride a bus, train or taxi alone.
    2. Ride with someone who just got his or her license.
    3. Ride a skateboard downtown during rush hour.
    4. Hitchhike to downtown or to another town.

Concerning drugs:
    1. Take only over-the-counter or prescription medicine.
    2. Smoke a cigarette if my friends were doing it.
    3. Try marijuana or alcohol once if I were sure I wouldn't get caught.
    4. Try crack or cocaine if I were sure I wouldn't get caught.

Concerning boyfriend/girlfriend:
    1. Try to be friends with many different people.
    2. Go steady with someone.
    3. Try to make out with someone on our first date.
    4. Have sex before marriage with someone who loves me.

Concerning recreation:
    1. Go running.
    2. Go roller-skating or skateboarding.
    3. Play tag in a busy shopping mall.
    4. Play tackle football without pads or participate in gymnastics without floor mats.

Concerning school:
    1. Give up an hour of doing something I like in order to study a little extra.
    2. Pass a secret note in class.
    3. Sleep during the study time right before a test.
    4. Skip school to do something fun with my friends.

Concerning entertainment:
    1. Watch television at home.
    2. Use my allowance to play video games for an hour at an arcade.
    3. Sneak into an R-rated movie.
    4. Go to a friend's party when his or her parents are on vacation.

To find your Risk Factor, add the numbers of the risks you've circled and compare that number with the scoring key below.
If your Risk Factor is:
    From 8 to 15—you take normal risks.
    From 16 to 22—you're taking a few foolish risks.
    From 23 to 28—you're in danger of hurting your life.
    From 29 to 32—you're in danger of destroying your life.

219

God's Risk-Takers Cards

✂

Saul is made king—1 Samuel 10:17-27	Saul's first victory—1 Samuel 11:6-13
Jonathan's battle—1 Samuel 14:4-14	Saul disobeys God—1 Samuel 15:1-11
David serves Saul—1 Samuel 16:14-23	David and Goliath—1 Samuel 17:45-51
Saul is jealous of David— 1 Samuel 17:57—18:9	Saul, Jonathan and David— 1 Samuel 19:1-7
Jonathan and David's oath— 1 Samuel 20:12-17	David spares Saul's life— 1 Samuel 24:1-11, 16-22
Saul goes to a witch—1 Samuel 28:1-20	The death of Saul and Jonathan— 2 Samuel 1:1-12

had. But the people wanted a ruler they could see, hear and touch, so God appointed a king to rule over them. At first, King Saul listened to the Lord and was a good king. But eventually he stopped doing God's will and did whatever he wanted.

So God asked Samuel the prophet to appoint a new king. His name was David. David's closest friend was Jonathan, Saul's son. The story of these men shows the results of both good and bad risk-taking.

220

Distribute Bibles, markers and the "God's Risk-Takers Cards" evenly among group members. If you have more than 12 kids, form teams. If you have fewer than 12 kids, give more than one card to some people. Have kids each read the scripture passage on their card(s) and decide if the person described took a good or a bad risk. Then ask each person (or team) to describe the situation in his or her passage.

Ask:

● **What's a common factor in the good risks each person took?**

● **What makes a bad risk bad?**

● **Which is easier: taking a bad risk or taking a good risk? Explain.**

Read aloud 1 Corinthians 6:19. Ask:

● **What's the most important reason we should avoid bad risks and take good risks?**

5. *Risky prayers*—(For each person you'll need a pencil and a 3×5 card.) Distribute 3×5 cards and pencils. Have kids each write one good risk they'll take on behalf of God or others, and one bad risk they'll try to avoid. Have the kids form a circle. Tell the group to say, "Lord, help me to risk . . ." Have a group member finish the sentence by reading the first thing listed on his or her card. Then have the group say, "Lord, help me avoid risking . . ." Have the same group member read the second item on his or her card to finish the sentence. Continue around the circle until kids each have read their card.

32 *TV and Me*

By Scott Koenigsaecker

Half of the junior highers in a recent Search Institute survey say they spend three or more hours each day watching television.

Television plays a central role in shaping what kids believe. Statistics say 83 percent of what we learn comes from what we see and 11 percent from what we hear. With audio-visual techniques, 85 percent can be recalled after three hours and 65 percent three days later. Impressive!

Use this meeting to help junior highers become more aware of what television tells them about their world, lifestyle, relationships and self-image.

OBJECTIVES

Participants will:
- play games to get them thinking about television;
- identify what they like and dislike about their top eight TV shows and how these shows resemble their lives;
- study Bible passages to understand God's view of our world, lifestyle, relationships and self-image;
- re-evaluate TV shows from God's point of view; and
- set goals for TV viewing.

BEFORE THE MEETING

Read the meeting, collect supplies and photocopy handouts. The week before the meeting have a couple of kids poll the other group members for their top five favorite TV shows. From the results, compile the eight best-liked shows your kids watch. Watch the top eight shows yourself so you'll be familiar with them.

Then, for activity #2, write the top eight shows on a sheet of newsprint. Also create a "TV Academy Awards" poster—a wall-size version of the "TV Ratings" handout, without the drawing of the television.

For each group of four to six, bring two sets of 32 circle-stickers—the first set one color and the second set another color—to use as TV dials in activities #2 and #4.

Also for each group of four to six, bring at least one Bible with a TV Guide cover wrapped around it to use in activity #3.

For the refreshment time (activity #6), bring a cake decorated like a TV set; and three round half-gallon containers of ice cream, each wrapped with construction paper with either the call letters ABC, NBC or CBS written on it.

Recruit kids' help in preparing for this meeting. For example, kids could:

● make the "TV Academy Awards" poster;

● bake and decorate the cake; and

● create the ABC, NBC and CBS ice cream covers.

Display the "TV Academy Awards" poster at the front of your meeting room.

THE MEETING

1. *TV Tag*—(You'll need a prize for the winner.) When the kids arrive, get them together for a game of TV Tag: In a confined area, kids try to not be tagged by the person who's "It." Kids run away from It or stoop down while yelling out the name of a TV show. Kids can only stay down five seconds. And when It catches someone, It goes to the sideline and cheers for the other players. The person who was caught becomes the new It. If you wish, limit the TV shows that may be yelled out according to type of show (for example, comedy, drama or cartoon); day of the week (for example, only Thursday night or Saturday); time of day (for example, 8 p.m. or 10 p.m.); or channel (for example, only shows on NBC, ABC or CBS). A show may be named only once. Award a prize to the last person tagged.

2. *Top five shows*—(You'll need the newsprint listing the top eight TV shows and the "TV Academy Awards" poster. For each person you'll need a "TV Ratings" handout and a pencil. For each group of four to six you'll need a set of 32 TV dials.) Have kids get into groups of four or six by getting together with other pairs. Add an adult sponsor to each group. Display the newsprint list of the top eight TV shows from last week's poll.

Have group members discuss what they like and dislike about each show. Then distribute the "TV Ratings" handouts and pencils. Explain the directions: Kids should write the top eight TV shows (from the newsprint list) in the boxes on the handout. Then they should mark the continuums to indicate how well the shows resemble their views about the world; the lifestyle they live; the type and quality of relationships they share with their parents, family, friends, strangers, enemies; and how their self-image compares to the image depicted in the main character(s) of the show.

Let group members discuss why they felt the shows did or didn't represent their lives, then average out their TV ratings for each show in each area.

Tell each group to choose an "anchorperson." Give each anchorperson that group's first set of 32 TV dials. Have the anchorpersons from the groups place their TV dials on the "TV Academy Awards" poster on the spots on the continuums that show the groups' averages.

Have the anchorpersons tell why their groups rated the different areas of the shows the way they did.

3. *Checking the guide* — (For each group of four to six you'll need a "God's TV Guide" handout, a pencil and at least one Bible with a TV Guide cover wrapped around it.) Say: **We've talked about what these TV shows tell us about viewing the world, our lifestyle, relationships and self-image. But as Christians, our primary guide for life is the Bible. Let's see how the Bible guides us in these four areas of life.**

Give each group a "God's TV Guide" handout and at least one Bible with a TV Guide cover wrapped around it. Tell groups to work through the handouts.

Bring groups together and have kids discuss their findings.

4. *Instant replay* — (For each group of four to six you'll need a second set of 32 different-color TV dials.) Give each group's anchorperson a second set of 32 different-color TV dials. Say: **Now that we understand more of God's view about**

TV Ratings

Instructions: For each show, circle the spots on the continuums that best represent how well the show resembles your view of the world, your lifestyle, your relationships and your self-image.

	just like me	not like me
View of world	0 5	10
Lifestyle	0 5	10
Relationships	0 5	10
Self-image	0 5	10

	just like me	not like me
View of world	0 5	10
Lifestyle	0 5	10
Relationships	0 5	10
Self-image	0 5	10

	just like me	not like me
View of world	0 5	10
Lifestyle	0 5	10
Relationships	0 5	10
Self-image	0 5	10

	just like me	not like me
View of world	0 5	10
Lifestyle	0 5	10
Relationships	0 5	10
Self-image	0 5	10

	just like me	not like me
View of world	0 5	10
Lifestyle	0 5	10
Relationships	0 5	10
Self-image	0 5	10

	just like me	not like me
View of world	0 5	10
Lifestyle	0 5	10
Relationships	0 5	10
Self-image	0 5	10

	just like me	not like me
View of world	0 5	10
Lifestyle	0 5	10
Relationships	0 5	10
Self-image	0 5	10

	just like me	not like me
View of world	0 5	10
Lifestyle	0 5	10
Relationships	0 5	10
Self-image	0 5	10

God's TV Guide

Instructions: For each section, read the Bible passage(s) and discuss the questions.

1. View of world—Romans 12:1-2

- How should we present or live our lives before God (verse 1)?
- What does the Bible mean when it uses the word "world" (verse 2)?
- Why should we be concerned about the influence of the world in our lives (verse 2)?
- What does it mean to be "transformed" (verse 2)?
- What does this passage say about God's will for us (verse 2)?

2. Lifestyle—Ephesians 4:22—5:5

- List the positive qualities and characteristics of our "new nature" as it's described in 4:25—5:1.
- List the things that a renewed person should "put off" or "put out" of his or her life (5:3-5).
- What does Ephesians 5:1 tell us are the goals of following Christ?

3. Relationships—1 John 4:7-11

- Who is the source of love (verse 1)?
- What is the command given to all Christians in verse 1?
- How do you define "love"?
- How did God show his love for us (verses 9-10)?

4. Self-image—Romans 12:3 and Genesis 1:27

- What kind of judgment should we have about ourselves according to Romans 12:3?
- What does it mean to be "sober"?
- We were not created in the image of any second-rate person . . . Whose image were we created in (Genesis 1:27)? What difference does that make in your life?

these areas, let's do an instant replay of our evaluation of the top eight TV shows—from God's point of view. On your "TV Ratings" handouts, mark squares on the continuums to rate each show based on what you just talked about. Discuss in your groups how the areas of the shows are the same or different compared to before. Then average out your new answers and have your anchorperson place the TV dials on the "TV Academy Awards" poster.

Comment on the similarities or differences of the two sets of TV dials. If both sets are the same, this indicates the kids' evaluations of the TV shows were, in both cases, done from a Christ-centered perspective.

If the second set of TV dials is significantly different, this indicates the kids discovered their perceptions are different from God's. And that they need to look at what they watch on television from a different point of view—God's point of view.

Praise kids in their discoveries either way. Encourage discussion about why the groups responded the way they did.

5. Commercial break—(For each person, you'll need the "TV Ratings" handout kids completed earlier and a pencil.) Have kids get their "TV Ratings" handouts and pencils again and sit in a circle. Have them each think about one goal they'd like to make about their TV watching. For example, someone may decide to stop watching a particular show; someone else may set a goal to talk about certain shows with other Christian friends; someone else may want to continue evaluating TV shows from a Christian viewpoint. Have kids each write their goal on the back of their handout.

Begin a circle prayer: "God, help us to . . ." Have kids fill in their goals, one by one, around the circle.

6. Refreshments—(You'll need the "TV" cake and the three ice cream containers.) Place the cake decorated like a TV and the containers of ice cream with the call letters on a table. Tell the "viewers" (kids) to pass through the line, get a piece of cake and then ask for a scoop of "ABC," "NBC" or "CBS."

Special Series: *By Daniel Raguse*

Sex Is for Marriage

It's a "bad news, good news" story.

The bad news:

One in five ninth-graders (20 percent) report having had sex already; and the rate for guys is more than double the rate for girls.

Eighty percent of today's unmarried males and 60 percent of unmarried females will have sex by age 19; and 40 percent of today's 14-year-olds will be pregnant at least once before they're 20.

Enough.

The good news:

Your youth group kids don't have to be statistics. They can beat the odds. They can enjoy their sexuality to the fullest—in the healthy, wholesome way God intends. With your help.

Use this special three-meeting series to help junior highers see why it's best to save sex for marriage. Show them God's instructions for the gift of sex; how and why to make wise decisions about sex; and how to say no to premarital sex.

HOW TO USE THIS SERIES

1. Carefully read this series and adapt it to your group's needs. Junior highers are at different levels of sexual maturity. Some may be interested, and others may have no interest in sex and little knowledge about it.

2. Decide which topics need emphasis and which are better left for another time. Homosexuality, pornography, AIDS and masturbation aren't covered in these meetings, but questions and concerns about these issues may arise.

3. Check with local schools and churches to find out what's being taught in sex-education programs.

4. Visit the library and read current information about sex topics. Be prepared with answers and resources.

5. Check with local clinics and health authorities for pamphlets and printed information to use as handouts. List local organizations or professionals as resources.

6. Because sex is a sensitive subject, meet with your junior highers' parents ahead of time. Tell them about the meetings' intentions and the importance of parental involvement.

7. Find guest speakers:

● (for meeting #1) a nurse, doctor or school psychologist—someone with experience in the field of sexual development. Ask this person to bring a baby, if possible, to emphasize the responsibility of sex.

● (for meeting #2) someone with experience working with unwed mothers or teenage mothers. A teenage mother (with an appropriate perspective) who'd feel comfortable talking with teenagers would be a good choice too.

● (for meeting #3) someone who has experienced sexual temptations but learned to say no. An older teenager might relate well to your junior highers.

If you can't find three guest speakers, get one who'll attend all three meetings.

At least two weeks before the meetings, tell your guest speakers the meeting topics, places and times. Tell them your questions and say that kids may ask questions too. Plan together that if a kid asks a question neither of you can answer, one of you will arrange to find the answer and report it later.

8. Find adult sponsors, preferably not group members' parents, who can attend the three kids' meetings. Brief them on each meeting's objectives and how they can help, particularly in small group activities.

9. Think about expanding the series by forming a support group for teenagers. (Instructions are in meeting #3, activity #6.) Get others in your church or community involved as discussion leaders or supporters.

In general, realize that during the meetings, sexually active junior highers may feel guilty or may just turn off. Lead this series with love and forgiveness. Remember how Jesus responded to the adulterous woman (John 8:1-11). Strive for his attitude: "Then neither do I condemn you. Go now and leave your life of sin."

33 *Instructions Included* (Meeting #1)

*T*he world shouts instructions about sex: "Go for it!" "Use sex to get your own way; it's a small price to pay." "Have sex and you'll be popular; you can go to all the best parties." "Everyone's doing it."

There's more. Kids believe the messages they hear. But the church's still, small voice saying, "Wait until after you're married; it's best that way," often gets muffled. Lost.

You can help turn down the world's voices. And turn up God's message.

Use this meeting to discuss with junior highers how the world's view of sex compares with God's view. Help them discover that sexuality is a gift containing joys and responsibilities.

OBJECTIVES

Participants will:
- review biological sex facts;
- identify sexual intercourse as a gift from God;
- examine God's instructions for using the gift of sex; and
- recognize how sex is misused in the world.

230

BEFORE THE MEETING

Read this meeting and "How to Use This Series" (page 227). Also read the entire three-part series before doing this first meeting. Collect supplies and photocopy handouts.

For activity #2, gather a small cardboard box (a shoe box works well) for every group of three or four.

For activity #3, create a question box by cutting a slot in the top of a small box covered with construction paper.

For activities #5 to #8, create four blank "Instructions for Using the Gift of Sex" forms, on newsprint (see example on page 233).

For activity #6, cut 10 to 15 slips of paper, each containing the name of a different TV show, magazine, song or movie that condones premarital sex.

Prepare snacks for activity #9.

Put "your questions" from activity #10 into the question box. Be sure your guest speaker knows the meeting topic, place and time (see page 228, step #7).

THE MEETING

1. Introduction—Welcome kids. Tell them this meeting is the first of three about sex. Say they may feel uneasy at times talking about sex, but ask them to give honest answers, ask tough questions and share concerns. Assure them no one will be put on the spot. Be aware that some kids may have a difficult time because of immaturity; others may feel guilty because of past experiences.

2. Box collages—(For each group of three or four, you'll need a small cardboard box, several magazines and newspapers, scissors, tape, glue, markers, construction paper, ribbon and other decorating materials.) Form groups of three or four people of the same sex. Have each group make a box collage by covering a small cardboard box with sexual images found in magazine and newspaper pictures and words. Provide each group with the supplies listed, including other decorating materials to decorate the boxes as gifts.

Get everyone together. Display the box collages and discuss the images. Say this meeting series covers more than the biological facts of sex; it explores choices teenagers make about sex, and the questions they have.

3. *Questions, questions*—(You'll need blank 3×5 cards, pencils and the question box.) Distribute 3×5 cards and pencils. Show kids the question box and explain that it's a method to answer kids' questions without embarrassing them. Say a guest speaker will appear at the end of each meeting to address questions about sex. Encourage kids to put their questions into the box before, during or after each meeting. Say the questions don't have to be signed and no one except the guest speaker will see them. If possible, make the box available during the week too.

4. *Following instructions*—(You'll need newsprint and a marker. For each person, you'll need a "What Do You See?" handout and a pencil.) Refer back to the box collages. Say they represent the God-given gift of sex. Read aloud 1 Corinthians 6:19-20. Say the gift of sex requires care and proper use.

Give kids each a "What Do You See?" handout. Have them attempt to complete it. After a few minutes, show the solution on newsprint. Discuss the importance of instructions. Tell examples: putting together a bicycle, building a model, building a desk.

THE SOLUTION

Say: **God's gift of sex comes with instructions, but many times his instructions aren't read or followed.**

5. *God's instructions*—(You'll need one of the four copies of the "Instructions for Using the Gift of Sex" and a marker.) Display the first blank newsprint instruction form.

Fill in "God" on the blank next to "Written by." Have kids help write God's instructions for sex on the form. Assign different people to read aloud the following Bible passages: Genesis 1:22; 4:1; Matthew 5:27-28; 19:3-6; 19:18; 1 Corinthians 7:1-2; Galatians 5:16-21; Ephesians 5:3; and 1 Thessalonians 4:3-5. Tell the group that fornication means having sex with someone you're not married to. Have the group supply the missing parts of the instruction form. Write their answers with a marker.

Emphasize that God intends sexual intercourse for marriage. Sex is a miracle that not only creates life, but expresses the oneness that married couples experience.

What Do You See?

Instructions: Connect the dots to reveal the picture.

Instructions for Using the Gift of Sex, Written by _____

● Use this gift to:

_____   _____   _____

● Use this gift if you: _____

● Using this gift as recommended can result in:

_____   _____   _____

_____   _____

6. *The media's instructions*—(You'll need another of the four copies of the "Instructions for Using the Gift of Sex" and a marker. You'll also need 10 to 15 slips of paper with names of TV shows, magazines, songs and movies written on them.) Display the second blank newsprint instruction form. Fill in "the Media" on the blank next to "Written by."

Get kids to think about the media's messages about sex by playing charades. Use the 10 to 15 paper slips with names of TV shows, magazines, songs and movies.

Discuss how the media influences attitudes toward sex. Have kids tell what they think the media's instructions for sex are.

7. *Peer pressure's instructions*—(You'll need the third of the four copies of the "Instructions for Using the Gift of Sex" and a marker.) Display the third blank newsprint instruction form. Fill in "Peer Pressure" on the blank next to "Written by."

Have the group stand in a circle. Say you're going to read some behaviors that sometimes result from peer pressure. For each behavior, have kids each step forward if they feel the behavior is good, step back if they feel the behavior is wrong, and stand still if they can't decide. Read:

● **using drugs**   ● **getting good grades**
● **gossiping**   ● **shoplifting**
● **going to youth group** ● **participating in sports**

- dressing a certain way
- listening to certain music
- going steady
- having sex
- joining school clubs
- getting a job
- eating certain foods
- dancing
- watching movies
- riding a skateboard
- doing service projects

Discuss how peer pressure can be both good and bad. Discuss the importance of judging behaviors. Have the group think of peer pressure's instructions for sex.

8. *Selfish desires' instructions*—(You'll need the last of the four copies of the "Instructions for Using the Gift of Sex" and a marker.) Display the fourth blank newsprint instruction form. Fill in "Selfish Desires" on the blank next to "Written by." Have kids sit in a circle. Say you're going to read a list of actions. For each action, have kids each stand if they feel the action is something they're old enough to do and sit if they feel it's something for older people. Read:

- working full time
- drinking alcohol
- cooking family meals
- owning a car
- planning meals
- serving jury duty
- traveling alone
- owning a house
- having children
- getting married
- living alone
- doing laundry
- maintaining lawns
- joining the military

Briefly talk about growing up. Ask what makes a person grown-up. Point out that wanting to be independent doesn't automatically mean you're ready to be. Say growing up means learning responsibility and respecting other people's needs. Ask how saving sex for after marriage fits being grown-up.

Have the group write instructions that selfish desires would give for sex.

9. *Refreshments*—(You'll need enough snacks for everyone.) Take a five-minute refreshment break. Prepare for the guest speaker.

10. *Sex questions*—(You'll need the question box with questions inside.) Get kids back together and introduce your speaker. Draw the questions from the question box (both yours and the kids') and have the speaker answer them. Let kids directly ask questions too.

Your questions:
- How does a woman become pregnant?
- Is it true you can't get pregnant during a period?
- Is it possible to get pregnant by French kissing or petting?

11. *Closing*—Form a circle. Go to each person and say: **(Name), God's given you the gift of sexuality. Use it to his glory and in accordance with his will.** You may make some small gesture as you address each person. For example, holding a hand, making the sign of the cross on his or her forehead, or even giving a small gift such as a bookmark or a sticker with an appropriate scripture passage on it. Read aloud 1 Corinthians 6:19-20 again and close with a prayer thanking God for his gift of sex. Ask for his forgiveness for sexual failures, and for strength to fight sexual temptations.

As kids head home, remind them to talk with their parents about this meeting.

34 Warning! Contents Could Explode (Meeting #2)

*L*ike most adults, junior highers have dreams,
goals and plans for a happy future. But unlike
adults, they don't have the ability to evaluate long-
term consequences of many behaviors. Too many
dreams are shattered by junior highers' unwise decisions to have sex, use drugs and drop out of school.

Use this meeting to help junior highers evaluate
the consequences of premarital sex and make wise
decisions about sexual behavior.

OBJECTIVES

Participants will:
- share their hopes and dreams for a future family;
- identify harmful consequences of premarital sex;
- compare arguments for having premarital sex to arguments against having premarital sex; and
- hear God's forgiveness for failures in sexual behavior.

BEFORE THE MEETING

Read the meeting, collect supplies and photocopy handouts.

For activity #1, gather a 2×4 piece of paper and a straight pin for each person.

On a sheet of newsprint, write the "Nine Effects of Premarital Sex on Marriage" information for activity #4.

Put "your questions" from activity #8 into the question box. Be sure your guest speaker knows the meeting topic, place and time.

THE MEETING

1. Looking ahead—(You'll need newsprint, masking tape and a marker. For each person you'll need a 2×4-inch piece of paper, a marker and a straight pin.) As group members arrive, tell them to imagine life when they're 40. Provide the 2×4 pieces of paper, markers and straight pins. Write the following five items on newsprint and tape it on the wall so kids can see. Have kids make name tags containing:

- their name;
- what their occupation will be;
- what their marital status will be;
- how many children they'll have (and whether they're boys or girls); and
- where they'll live.

Have everyone sit in a circle, and have kids each describe their future life.

2. Hopes and dreams—Discuss the pressure to grow up. Talk about hopes and dreams. Then tell kids to get comfortable. Read aloud these stories of two people whose dreams didn't come true.

> **Jan:** At 14, Jan is very involved at school. She's a member of the school choir and girls' basketball team. She's an honor student. Her father is a doctor. Her mother owns a gift shop. Jan dreams of becoming a fashion designer. She goes to church about twice a month, but isn't active in her youth group. Two months ago, Jan went to a school dance and left with a high school junior. She felt popular. That night she had sex. Today she found out she's pregnant. "I can't be," she says. "I only did it that one time."

> **Lee:** Lee is 35. He's been married three months to a woman he met a year ago. Lee has been sexually active since age 13. He's never gotten a girl pregnant nor acquired a sexually transmitted disease. But Lee has suffered a great deal from having sex with many women. He compares his wife's sexual performance with others'. He feels guilty about his past, so he doesn't enjoy sex. His wife doesn't know about his past. They don't communicate. Today they decided to separate. Lee figures divorce is the easy way out.

Discuss how these stories tell an important truth—that sometimes dreams don't come true. But sad stories don't have to end sad.

Ask:

What can Jan and Lee do now that they realize their mistakes?

Read aloud 1 John 1:9 and Matthew 11:28-29. Discuss how God's forgiveness and protection cover all of life's sorrows.

3. *Consequences*—(For each person, you'll need a "The Then-What Tree" handout and a pencil.) Say that the next activity looks at possible consequences of premarital sex.

Hand out copies of the "The Then-What Tree" and pencils. Tell group members to fill in the rectangles by following different branches of the tree, starting at the bottom. Encourage them to try different branches and fill in all the rectangles.

After a few minutes, get everyone in a circle and have kids share answers. Talk about the feeling boxes. Compare the consequences of saying no to premarital sex to those of saying yes. Discuss how sometimes the "no" consequence looks worse, but in the end it's a better choice.

4. *Effects of premarital sex*—(You'll need the newsprint entitled "Nine Effects of Premarital Sex on Marriage." For each person you'll need a Bible and a marker.) Form groups of four to six. Display the "Nine Effects of Premarital Sex on Marriage" newsprint. Have group members each write on the back of their name tag how premarital sex could affect their future family. Make Bibles available. Have kids read aloud the four scripture passages listed below the nine points. In their groups, have them choose and write the one verse that comforts them most as they think about their future.

5. *The debate*—(For each person you'll need "The Great Sex Debate" handout.) Give each person "The Great Sex Debate" handout. Assign groups of one to three kids different arguments from the handout. Instruct the groups to think of rebuttals to their assigned arguments. Encourage them to use the scripture passages, the "Nine Effects of Premarital Sex on Marriage" and their own debating skills. Tell each group to select one person to be the debater taking the position: "Premarital sex is wrong."

While group members are working, choose a few convincing kids to debate for premarital sex. Tell them to support the specif-

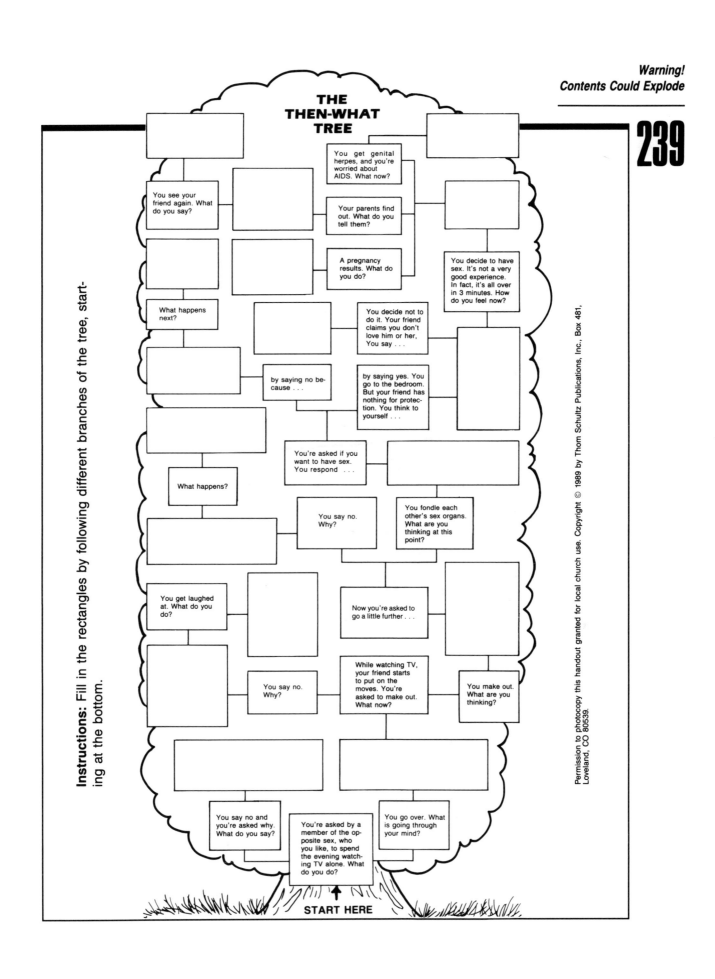

THE THEN-WHAT TREE

Instructions: Fill in the rectangles by following different branches of the tree, starting at the bottom.

You get genital herpes, and you're worried about AIDS. What now?

You see your friend again. What do you say?

Your parents find out. What do you tell them?

A pregnancy results. What do you do?

You decide to have sex. It's not a very good experience. In fact, it's all over in 3 minutes. How do you feel now?

What happens next?

You decide not to do it. Your friend claims you don't love him or her. You say . . .

by saying no because . . .

by saying yes. You go to the bedroom. But your friend has nothing for protection. You think to yourself . . .

You're asked if you want to have sex. You respond . . .

What happens?

You say no. Why?

You fondle each other's sex organs. What are you thinking at this point?

You get laughed at. What do you do?

Now you're asked to go a little further . . .

You say no. Why?

While watching TV, your friend starts to put on the moves. You're asked to make out. What now?

You make out. What are you thinking?

You say no and you're asked why. What do you say?

You're asked by a member of the opposite sex, who you like, to spend the evening watching TV alone. What do you do?

You go over. What is going through your mind?

START HERE

240

Nine Effects of Premarital Sex on Marriage

Instructions: Write these on a sheet of newsprint and tape it on the wall.

If you have premarital sex, you're likely to:
(1) break up with your partner before you marry him or her.
(2) scare off anyone who wants to marry a virgin.
(3) be less happy in your marriage.
(4) get a divorce.
(5) commit adultery after you marry.
(6) be fooled into marrying for the wrong reason.
(7) achieve married-sex happiness more quickly, but
(8) be less satisfied with your married sex life.
(9) totally spoil sex due to conditioned feelings of guilt and remorse.

(Taken from *Sex, Love, or Infatuation* by Ray Short, copyright 1978 Augsburg Publishing House.)

Scripture Passages of Comfort as You Face the Future
● Psalm 46:7   ● Matthew 6:31-33   ● John 16:33   ● 1 Corinthians 2:9

The Great Sex Debate

Instructions: Use this sheet to prepare for your debate.

Arguments Supporting Premarital Sex
● It tests sex before marriage.
● It shows love.
● It gives the pleasures of marriage without the responsibilities.
● The world could blow up before I have a chance to do it.
● Everyone's doing it.
● We're going to get married anyway.
● Birth control takes away the dangers.
● It prevents loneliness.

Scripture Passages Rebutting Arguments for Premarital Sex
● Genesis 1:22   ● Genesis 4:1   ● Matthew 5:27-28   ● Matthew 19:3-6
● Matthew 28:20   ● 1 Corinthians 6:13, 18   ● 1 Corinthians 7:1-4
● 1 Corinthians 13:4-5   ● Galatians 5:16-21   ● Ephesians 5:3   ● Ephesians 5:17
● 1 Thessalonians 4:3-5   ● Hebrews 13:4   ● 1 Peter 5:8   ● 1 John 2:15-17

ic arguments from the newsprint but not to overdo it.

When everyone's ready, set up two-minute debates. Allow each side one minute to state arguments for its position. Follow the order of the statements. Have the debaters arguing for premarital sex go first; those arguing against, second.

6. Forgiveness—Have everyone sit in a circle. Ask group members if they know kids in their school who are sexually active. (Realize that some in your group may themselves be active.) Discuss the feelings that many teenagers have after intercourse—guilt, fear, confusion, depression. Say such feelings are signs that a behavior is wrong. But God stands ready to forgive and help.

Briefly tell the story of David and Bathsheba, 2 Samuel 11—12. Explain how the consequence of their adultery was severe—the death of their first child. But God didn't desert David. Read aloud 2 Samuel 12:24. Show how God blessed them with another child, conceived in love. Read aloud Romans 5:3-5, a word of encouragement and hope.

7. Refreshments—(You'll need snacks for everyone.) Use this break to prepare for the guest speaker.

8. Sex questions—(You'll need the question box.) Get kids back together. Introduce your speaker. Have your guest address questions in the question box first, and then any asked directly by the kids.

Your questions:
● What are the best ways to prevent pregnancy?
● Can you get venereal disease by kissing?
● How do you know if you're pregnant?
● How can you be sure you don't have a sexually-transmitted disease if you've had intercourse?

9. Closing—Conclude with a prayer asking God for strength to resist the world's pressures.

35 *Fragile: Handle With Care*

(Meeting #3)

*I*t's hard to say no when it means going against the crowd. Taking a stand against peers requires strength, courage and skill. Recently, however, public campaigns have helped show junior highers they can refuse to drink or use drugs and still be accepted.

Use this meeting to give junior highers the skill and encouragement to say no to premarital sex.

OBJECTIVES

Participants will:
- identify conditions and environments that diffuse or promote sexual temptation;
- develop a personal set of sexual standards that prohibits premarital sex; and
- have an opportunity to create a personal support group for dealing with sexual concerns.

BEFORE THE MEETING

Read the meeting, collect supplies and photocopy handouts.

For activity #1, gather paper, cardboard, tape, rubber bands, tissue paper and foam rubber for packaging materials. Bring enough uncooked eggs for everyone. Also gather assorted colored stickers and an "eggsellent" award, such as a colored, hard-boiled egg or an Egg McMuffin coupon.

Try activity #1 prior to the meeting. Be sure you have cleaning supplies handy to take care of broken eggs.

For activity #2, gather red, yellow and green crayons—enough for each person to have one of each.

For refreshment time (activity #7), bring a "delicate dessert," such as cream puffs.

Remind your guest speaker of the meeting topic, place and time. Put your questions from activity #8 into the question box.

THE MEETING

1. ***Packaging the gift***—(You'll need a large plastic dropcloth. For each person you'll need an assortment of colorful stickers and a marker. Each person will also need an egg and assorted packaging materials, such as paper, cardboard, tape, rubber bands, tissue paper and foam rubber. For the winner of the drop contest you'll need an "eggsellent" award.) Give each group member an egg and say to package the egg to protect it from breaking. Explain what you're going to do with the packaged eggs. Provide packaging materials.

Let kids decorate their packaging with stickers and markers. Then have a drop contest. Lay down a plastic dropcloth. Begin the contest by having kids drop their eggs from 6 inches. Then 12, then 18, and higher until only one egg isn't broken. Give the winner an "eggsellent" award, such as a colored, hard-boiled egg or an Egg McMuffin coupon.

Discuss with group members how God's gift of sex is much more precious than the egg—and can easily break when God's protective instructions are disobeyed. Read aloud 1 Corinthians 6:19-20 as an opening focus.

2. ***Danger zones***—(For each person you'll need a "What's Dangerous?" handout and three crayons: red, yellow and green.) Give kids each the "What's Dangerous?" handout and a red, a yellow and a green crayon. Say: **The gift of sex is constantly being threatened by temptation. But sex needs special care and handling. We have the choice to fight off temptation or place ourselves in danger.**

Have kids complete the handout.

Discuss the group's responses. Talk about unsafe places for resisting sexual temptation. Remind the group of God's promise of help in 1 Corinthians 10:13.

244

What's Dangerous?

Instructions: When are sexually tempting situations dangerous? For each of the following situations, color in the traffic light RED if it's so dangerous you should stop it; YELLOW if it's somewhat dangerous and you should proceed with caution; or GREEN if it's safe to go ahead without being sexually tempted.

Situation	Rating
Being under the influence of drugs	
Going to an unsupervised party	
Going on a group date	
Being alone with a person of the opposite sex at your house when nobody else is home	
Being unchaperoned with a person of the opposite sex in a movie theater	
Going to a supervised party	
Going to a school dance with friends	
Going to a basketball game with a person of the opposite sex	
Leaving a school dance with a member of the opposite sex to sit in a car	
Walking home after school with a person of the opposite sex	
Meeting a person of the opposite sex at the park late at night	
Meeting a person of the opposite sex at a restaurant	

3. ***How to say no***—(You'll need newsprint and a marker.) Have everyone sit in a circle. Have kids brainstorm different ways to say no. Write ideas on newsprint. Some examples: "I'm sorry, but no"; "I'm not that kind of guy"; "No way, José"; "Sorry Charlie"; "N.O., No"; "That's not me"; "NOPE"; "Don't even think about it."

Have each person pick a favorite "no" answer. Use the answers in the game, Honey, If You Love Me, Smile. Choose one person to be "It." Have that person go to someone in the circle and say in a convincing manner, "Honey, if you love me, won't you please just smile?" The person responding shouldn't smile and should give his or her "no" answer. For example, "I love you, Honey, but no way, José!" The one who's It should keep trying until he or she makes the person smile or tries three times. He or she must then move on to the next person. Whoever smiles is It.

Discuss how repeatedly saying no is the key to not giving in. Once your mind is made up, saying no isn't really that hard.

4. ***When to say no***—(For each person, you'll need a "Steps to Sex" handout and a pencil.) Give kids each a "Steps to Sex" handout and pencil. Explain the directions and have kids complete their handouts.

Discuss the safety limits kids determine. Say that going no further than these limits assures a person of using God's gift of sex as God desires. Tell how setting limits ahead of time makes it easier when it's time to say no. Discuss how different levels of intimacy with a boyfriend or girlfriend take you to different steps; only marriage should allow a trip near the top.

5. ***Putting it all together***—(You'll need newsprint and a marker.) Form groups of four to six. Print the following on newsprint: Danger Zones; How and When to Say No; Possible Consequences; Comfort.

Read aloud the three situations on page 247 one at a time to the group. For each situation have small groups determine:
 ● the danger zones;
 ● how and when "no" should've been said;
 ● what the possible consequences are; and
 ● what comfort can be given.
Write their suggestions on newsprint.
Read aloud Ephesians 6:13-18 to wrap up the activity.

246

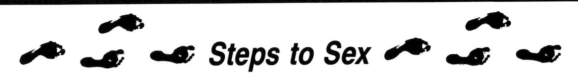

Steps to Sex

Instructions: Use this sheet to help you set a personal limit for the steps to sex. First, read the eight "Sex Check Questions." Then for each step, starting at the bottom, ask yourself the questions. When you answer "yes" to any question, that step may be your safety limit. Put a check mark on that step.

Sex Check Questions
1. Is my conscience telling me to stop?
2. Do I feel lust (the desire to have intercourse)?
3. Am I being controlled or used by others?
4. Do I feel guilty?
5. Will this cause me to be dishonest with parents or friends?
6. Does this show respect and care for the other person?
7. Could this have a negative consequence?
8. Is this a misuse of God's gift of sex?

The Step to Stop

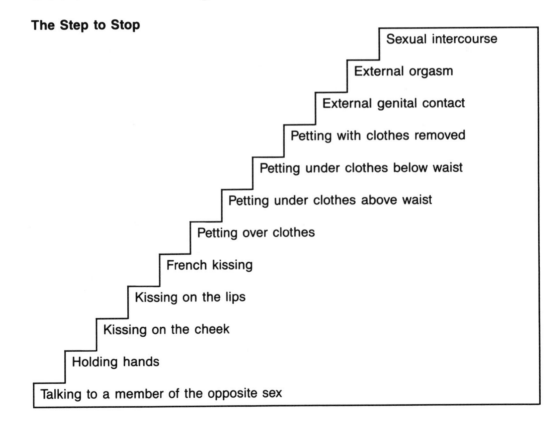

Sexual intercourse
External orgasm
External genital contact
Petting with clothes removed
Petting under clothes below waist
Petting under clothes above waist
Petting over clothes
French kissing
Kissing on the lips
Kissing on the cheek
Holding hands
Talking to a member of the opposite sex

1. Dawn, a seventh-grade girl, goes to a slumber party with friends. After the adults are asleep, the girls get into the liquor cabinet. Dawn has too much to drink. She calls her boyfriend and asks him to come over. Though the rest of the girls tell her not to do it, Dawn sneaks out. She's in her nightgown, and her boyfriend wants to make out with her. They go out behind the garage where they eventually have sex.

2. Joel is a mature-looking eighth-grader. One night while riding his bike, he meets Julie, a local high school senior. They hit it off and she asks him to go to the drive-in later. She offers to drive. He goes wild with the thought of going out with a senior. He tells his parents he's going to a school dance, and if it lasts longer than midnight, he'll call. Julie picks him up at the corner. In a short time they're making out at the drive-in. Julie asks Joel if he's ever done it. He lies and says yes. Before he knows it, Julie is undressing him. He feels uncomfortable, but doesn't want to look stupid. After a few awkward moments, he asks if she's taking the pill. She laughs and says she is. They have sex. Afterward, Joel feels terrible. He looks at his watch. It's 12:45.

3. Dan and Jean, both ninth-graders, have been going steady for three months. They've only kissed so far, but now Dan wants more. Jean doesn't feel it's right but she doesn't want to lose Dan. One afternoon, she invites Dan over to her house knowing that her parents won't come home for at least two hours. Dan suggests they go up to her bedroom. As they make out, he tells her he loves her. He starts unbuttoning her blouse. Jean hesitates. But she's so happy Dan loves her, she gives in. As things get heated, Jean finds herself enjoying Dan's touch and decides to make him feel good too. Before they can stop themselves, they're lying on the bed nude. All of a sudden, a door opens downstairs.

6. *Support group*—Have everyone sit in a circle. Discuss the possibility of a teenage sexual support group. See "Starting a Teenage Sex Support Group" on page 248.

If group members choose to have a support group, tell them it will take dedication and commitment. You may want to write some kind of contract. To plan your first meeting, you may want to secure the help of your pastor, a local child psychologist or other professionals.

7. *Refreshments*—(You'll need dessert for everyone.) Celebrate this final meeting with a "delicate dessert" such as cream puffs. Also use this time to prepare for your final guest speaker.

248

Starting a Teenage Sex Support Group

Instructions: Let these steps help you get a sex support group for kids started in your church.

1. Present the support group as an option to be voted on by the kids.

2. Discuss what a support group could offer:
   - a place for kids to talk with other kids for support or help;
   - a place to get adult help in an emergency;
   - a place to learn more about sexual maturity;
   - continuation of the question box;
   - more guest speakers;
   - studies on sexuality issues, such as homosexuality, abortion and AIDS;
   - a group that promotes "No Sex Before Marriage";
   - a newsletter of information and support;
   - an opportunity to write letters to lawmakers, TV programmers and school officials about sexual issues of concern; and
   - sex-ed nights sponsored for the church or community.

3. Discuss when and where meetings could take place.

4. Have kids list possible adult leaders.

5. Discuss a possible name for the group; for example, TAPS (Teenagers Against Premarital Sex).

6. Elect youth officers to help adults plan programs.

8. *Sex questions*—(You'll need the question box.) Get kids back together. Introduce the speaker. Have your guest address the questions in the question box first, then any asked directly by the kids.

Your questions:
- Won't saying no make me lose my boyfriend/girlfriend?
- Whose responsibility is it to say no—the guy's or girl's?
- Why is it harder for a guy to say no?
- Is it okay to reach sexual climax as long as intercourse doesn't take place?

9. *Closing*—Close with a prayer asking God to give group members the wisdom and strength to use his gift of sex in a good way. End by having a group member read aloud 1 Corinthians 6:19-20.

Remind kids to talk with their parents about this meeting.